Fifty Easy
Old-Fashioned Roses,
Climbers, and
Vines

Fifty Easy Old-Fashioned Roses, Climbers, and Vines

Anne M. Zeman

Henry Holt and Company.
New York

Henry Holt and Company, Inc.
Publishers since 1866
115 West 18th Street
New York, New York 10011

Henry Holt® is a registered
trademark of Henry Holt and Company, Inc

Published in Canada by Fitzhenry & Whiteside Ltd.,
195 Allstate Parkway, Markham, Ontario L3R 4T8.

Library of Congress Cataloging-in-Publication Data

Zeman, Anne M.
Fifty easy old-fashioned roses, climbers, and vines / Anne M. Zeman. — 1st ed.
p.   cm.
"An Irving Place Press book" — T.p. verso
Includes index.
1. Old roses. 2. Ornamental climbing plants—Heirloom varieties.
3. Rose culture. 4. Gardening I. Title.
SB411.65.055Z45   1995   95-9096
635.9'33372—dc20   CIP
ISBN 0-8050-3979-1

First Edition—1995

AN IRVING PRESS PLACE BOOK
Designed by Charlotte Staub

Printed in Hong Kong
All first editions are printed on acid-free paper. ∞

1 3 5 7 9 10 8 6 4 2

For Mark and Mom

ACKNOWLEDGMENTS

Gardening is a shared experience: the sharing of knowledge, plants, and time. Many people were kind enough to share these things with me as I researched, wrote, and gathered photographs for this book:

Michelle Haynes, lifelong friend and fellow gardener, who always has time to discuss the merits and difficulties of plants, and who traveled with me to many of the gardens and nurseries where we studied and photographed flowers for this book.

Charles Cresson, an extraordinary plantsman, who was kind enough to review the manuscript and suggest ways to make the book better.

Kate Kelly, my friend and partner, whose editorial and professional skills are without equal.

Many thanks, too, to Ray Roberts for his enthusiastic support and guidance, to Ben Ratliff for his attention to detail, and to Charlotte Staub for creating a beautiful book design.

My family was very supportive during writing of this book, particularly my husband, Mark, who constantly encourages me to install new gardens to reduce his lawnmowing time. And gratitude must also be expressed to my faithful feline companion, Libby, who slept in my lap through much of the writing this book.

I would also like to thank the following people who generously shared their photography: Liz Ball, Kathy Wilkinson Barash, Charles Cresson, Michelle Haynes, Mike Lowe, Jack Potter, and Mike Shoup.

Contents

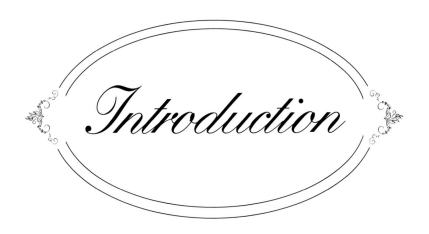

OLD ROSES

All roses are beautiful, but old roses possess a unique beauty, not to mention a shining versatility. Unlike modern Hybrid Teas, old roses come in an astonishing array of flower forms, colors, and sizes. Old roses come in all shapes—singles, doubles, and quartered—some with five petals, some with fifteen, or even with one hundred! Buds open into round cup-shapes that, unlike Hybrid Teas, become more beautiful as they unfold and mature. Old roses bloom in colors from the clearest pinks to the deepest crimsons, and in every shade in between. There are also pure whites and a few yellows.

The fragrance of the old roses is also astonishing—and truly intoxicating. Scents range from sweet to fruity, musky to spicy. Although some have only light scents, almost all old roses are fragrant.

As with flower forms and fragrance, old roses display a wide array of growth habits. Unlike the small, compact Hybrid Teas, old roses include plants as small as two or three feet and climbers that grow as tall as 30 feet. Thus, old-fashioned roses can grace virtually every corner of a lawn or garden, from the formal rose beds to foundation plantings, to climbing over a trellis or on a tree.

An old rose is generally defined as one grown before the first Hybrid Tea was developed in 1867. The majority of roses chosen for this book fit this definition. I have included a few more recent roses that date since 1867 because of their overall beauty and grace, but no rose is later than 1900. No hybrid teas are included.

Old roses and climbers are relatively easy to grow. Many thrive on neglect, as evidenced by the long-forgotten varieties performing beautifully in old cemeteries or abandoned sites. The fifty roses selected for this book need little more than a well-prepared hole for planting and pruning once a year.

TYPES OF ROSES

The old garden roses are classified into different types of historic classes, which are refered to throughout the text.

Gallica Roses. Dating back more than 3,000 years, Gallica roses are considered the oldest of all garden roses. Gallicas grow wild in western Europe.

They are very hardy and adaptable and thrive in poor soil. Very fragrant roses, Gallicas flower only once each year, in pink to crimson and purple to lavender on compact, dense shrubs. Gallica roses are also known as the French rose or the "Rose of Provins."

Damask Roses. Known for their exquisite fragrance, Damask roses were named for Damascus, Syria, where the rose was first documented. Spanish missionaries introduced them to North America, where they were known as the "Rose of the Castile." Damasks flower in a rather loose formation, and bloom in masses of red, pink, or white flowers early in the season. 'Autumn Damask' blooms again in the fall.

Alba Roses. Dating back to the Middle Ages, Alba roses are one of the most beautiful of the old roses and one of the hardiest, thriving under difficult conditions and needing minimum care. Alba roses are always white or the palest pink and possess a sweet scent. They grow in large bushes with few thorns and bloom once in early summer.

Centifolia Roses. Also known as Cabbage roses or Provence roses, Centifolia roses have up to one hundred petals in each flower. Centifolias appeared around the end of the sixteenth century. They form large bushes with full-blooming, double flowers in white and all shades of pink. Centifolias are known for their intense, rich fragrance, which is still used in the French perfume industry.

Moss Roses. Moss roses appeared unexpectedly around 1700 as a mutation of *Rose centifolia.* Noted for their unique moss-like growth, these roses develop a thick green or brown covering of scented glands on their unopened buds and flower stems. Moss roses have an attractive, arching habit. Blooms come in all shades of pink and white. They bloom in early summer; some varieties bloom again in late summer.

China Roses. Cultivated in China for many centuries before being introduced to Europe in 1792, China roses became extremely popular because they were nearly everblooming. 'Old Blush' (also known as 'Parson's Pink China') and 'Slater's Crimson China' were the first to be brought to England and France in 1792 and 1793, respectively. China roses are dwarf, perpetual-flowering plants with blooms in red, pink, or white in single or loosely double flowers with a slightly fragrant scent. China roses are also called Bengal roses.

Tea Roses. The Tea rose is a hybrid that occurred long ago in China and was first introduced into Europe around 1810. Ever-blooming in pink, cream, buff, and light yellow, Tea roses are loose, open-cupped, and sweet-scented. They were the first roses to feature long, pointed buds. The leaves, when crushed, have a tea scent. Forming slender bushes about 2 to 3 feet high, Tea roses are extremely long-lived plants, and many are highly disease-resistant. A new class of Tea roses was bred by crossing Teas with Bourbons and Noisettes. This class became the modern Hybrid Tea.

Noisette Roses. John Champney of Charleston, South Carolina, crossed a China rose and a Musk rose to create 'Champney's Pink Cluster.' Philippe Noisette, a French nurseryman who lived in Charleston created 'Blush Noisette' from one of Champney's seedlings. Noisette sent seeds to his brother in Paris, who dubbed them Noisette roses. Noisette roses originally had small flowers and bloomed in colors from white to pink and crimson to purple. European hybriders crossed these small Noisettes with larger-flowered Tea roses, thus developing Noisettes with larger blossoms and an expanded range of colors, but reduced hardiness. (In North America, Noisettes are hardy to Zone 7).

Portland Roses. Introduced around 1800, Portland roses were the first new group of hybrids created by crossing old European roses and new Chinese introductions. Named Portland after Margaret Cavendish Bentinck, 2nd Duchess of Portland, these roses are known for their gorgeous pinks, and rich, red blooms. Portlands are intensely fragrant, and the full-petaled blossoms are valued for their late-flowering habit.

Bourbon Roses. Bourbon roses appeared around 1820, about the same time as the Noisettes. They were named for Bourbon Island (now known as Réunion Island) in the southern Indian Ocean. On the island, rose bushes were grown as thick hedges. A visiting French botanist discovered in a hedge a seedling which was a hybrid between the two common roses, 'Parson's Pink China' and 'Autumn Damask.' He sent seeds from this hybrid back to Paris. From that seed came the original Bourbon roses, which were painted by Redouté in 1824. The pink blooms are repeat flowering and have a strong, heady fragrance.

Hybrid Perpetuals. Hybrid Perpetuals resulted from a complex of marriages in the 1800s between the Chinas and Portlands, then the Bourbons and Noisettes, and eventually, the Teas. Immensely popular in nineteenth-century gardens and used extensively for cut flowers, Hybrid Perpetuals bloom in red, mauve, pink, and white. Large and full-petaled, these roses produce a mass of flowers in early summer followed by occasional blooms during the rest of the season. Hybrid Perpetuals became the parents of a new group—the modern Hybrid Teas of today.

Rugosa Roses. Known for their hardiness, Rugosas are disease-resistant plants that need almost no care. They are drought-tolerant and will grow in sandy soil or in the salt spray at the seashore. Rugosa roses have magnificent foliage, beautiful flowers, and showy hips. Most are repeat-flowering with uniquely ribbed and veined foliage.

Caring for roses is not difficult. Once planted, roses need only an hour of tending per plant per season. Success is as simple as preparing good soil and providing lots of sunshine. Choose a location with at least six hours of sun a day, for only a few roses bloom well in partial shade, that is, approximately four hours of sun. Despite their need for abundant sun, roses do best if shaded from the hottest afternoon sun.

Roses tolerate a wide variety of soil conditions. Ideal soil is neutral to slightly acid, and well-drained. Roses adapt to most soils, but test your soil and amend it accordingly. Soil in western states frequently is too alkaline, and in eastern states too acid. Sulphur or lime may be needed to amend these conditions. The ground should be dug 18 to 24 inches deep. Add plenty of compost and rotted manure. Plant roses as soon as they arrive, making sure the roots are kept moist until they are in the ground. When planting roses, dig a large hole about 12 to 14 inches deep and 12 to 15 inches wide—and add another spadeful of compost and manure. The bud, or swelling at the base of the plant, should be set level with the ground. Mound up the soil in the hole so the roots can spread out over the mound. Put in additional soil carefully around the roots, leaving no open spaces. When the hole is nearly filled, water thoroughly; after the water has soaked in, add additional soil and water. Plant roses 18 to 24 inches apart, and 6 to 8 feet apart for climbers.

To maintain your roses, use a general garden fertilizer of 15-15-15 in early spring, again when buds appear, and again in mid-season—simply remember to fertilize on the first of May, June, and July. Water weekly and at least one inch deep. It is better to water deeply once a week than to water at short intervals several times a week. To prevent fungus diseases, water at the base of the plant and avoid wetting the foliage. If using overhead sprinklers, water during the day so surface moisture evaporates. Spread 2 to 4 inches of mulch to keep moisture in and keep weeds out. For winter protection in frost areas, mound up mulch about 6 or 12 inches high around the bases of the plants.

Most roses should be pruned in late winter or early spring before buds appear. All dead wood should be removed and canes should be cut back to about half of the previous season's growth. Any special requirements or additional recommendations on pruning are listed in the description sections for each rose entry.

CLIMBING ROSES

Climbing roses are not a distinct class of roses, but are tall-growing roses from the major rose groups. Their long canes stretch along fences, weave around trellises and arbors, and clamber up pillars. They grow at various heights and come in the same array of colors as the old roses. Because they are old roses, they have a much broader range of habits than modern climbers.

Climbing roses do not literally "climb," but grow as other roses do. Unlike vines, they do not have tendrils or aerial roots with which to cling to surfaces. Instead, they need some help. For this reason, climbing roses require extra care. Supports, such as trellises, arbors, or pillars, are needed to provide support and canes will have to be trained.

TRAINING

Climbers have varying growth habits. Some grow upright and with stiff canes that are difficult to bend and train. These roses are best grown on pillars. Other climbers are more flexible and can be used to cover trellises, walls, and fences. When training climbers, it's best to start early. Arbors should have small gaps between supports; if not, attach thin, sturdy wires to provide additional support. If growing roses on a house or garage, hammer galvanized nails into the wall the rose will grow on, then wrap 16-gauge galvanized wire around each nail, creating a vertical line of wire connecting the nails. Begin training the rose as soon as it reaches the first vertical bend or nail. Secure it loosely to the wire with soft twine or green plastic ties. As the rose develops through the summer, continue bending back the young canes and secure them in place.

PRUNING

Climbers need little pruning. The main reason to prune is to remove dead or old canes that no longer produce flowers. Pruning is also needed to keep the roses within reasonable bounds, to shape the plants, or to thin them out when they become too dense.

Prune climbers that flower on new wood in early spring before budding. Cut back the major canes to about three or four buds.

Prune roses that bloom on old wood just after they finish blooming. Old stems at or near ground level will need to be taken out periodically to encourage the development of new growth.

Prune dead or diseased growth at any time.

VINES

A perfect partner for climbing roses, vines are planted to intermingle with roses growing along the sides of houses or up porch pillars. Vines come in a variety of different flower shapes, colors, and fragrances, and many have brilliant fall foliage. Some have attractive—even edible—fruit. Several are evergreen and provide year-round interest or cover.

Vines were used much more often in times gone by. Perhaps the screen they created from the hot sun made them a necessity before air conditioning. And many people today hold the mistaken idea that vines are difficult to grow.

The cultivation of vines is no more difficult than that of most plants, and unlike climbing roses, many vines will climb by themselves. All climbing plants need some kind of support to grow on, but often the most difficult task is getting the trellis home in the car.

Annual vines, such as morning glories, deserve a place in every garden because of their quick growth and showy blooms. Annuals grow, flower, and produce fruit in a single growing season and will have to be replanted again the following year. Perennial vines, such as clematis, grow, flower, and die back to the ground each year and sprout again each following spring. Woody vines, such as wisteria, go dormant in the winter and regrow each year from buds along stems.

A variety of vines serve a multitude of uses, from covering bare walls and fences to creating quick-growing privacy screens. Vines also provide color for arbors, pergolas, and trellises, and create summer shade when grown on overhead structures or along porch rails. They also make quick-growing ground-covers. Whatever use you choose, there is a vine for most every surface.

—Anne M. Zeman

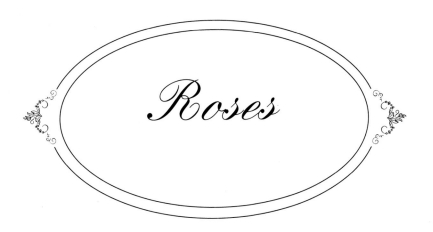

Roses

'Alfred de Dalmas'

TYPE: Moss

PARENTAGE: Unknown

INTRODUCED: 1855 by Portemer, France

 HISTORY

The name 'Alfred de Dalmas' is used interchangeably with 'Mousseline' to describe this Moss rose. In the United States, 'Alfred de Dalmas' is the name more commonly used. Generally thought to be related to 'Autumn Damask' or 'Quartre Saisons Blanc,' 'Alfred de Dalmas,' like all Moss roses, is a Centifolia that has growth on its sepals that resembles moss. Bred between 1850 and 1870, Moss roses were quite popular with the Victorians.

'Alfred de Dalmas' is the best repeat flowering Moss rose. Medium-size flowers are 2½ to 3 inches across, in a pale blush pink, which fades to white. The delicately-scented blooms are cup-shaped, with high centers, and semi-double in form with 55 to 65 petals. Borne in tight clusters, the blooms of 'Alfred de Dalmas' are quite free-flowering. The moss is greenish-brown, turning to red-brown on older stems. Growth is compact and bushy, reaching 3 to 4 feet high, spreading about 2 to 3 feet. Foliage is pale green-gray with round, spoon-shaped leaves. The canes are rough, but have few thorns. 'Alfred de Dalmas' is tolerant of poor soils, disease resistant, and winter hardy.

BLOOM TIME: Mid June with good repeat bloom in the fall.
Often blooms continuously from June through October.

USES: Because of the compactness of the bush, 'Alfred de Dalmas' is perfect for smaller gardens. It makes an exceptional low hedge and a charming specimen plant in rose gardens or in containers.

POSITION: Sun or part shade.

ZONES: 4 to 9.

'Baronne Prévost'

TYPE: Hybrid Perpetual
PARENTAGE: Unknown
INTRODUCED: 1842 by Desprez, France

 HISTORY

Raised by Desprez of Yébles, France, 'Barron Prévost' is named for the sister of Desprez's friend, Guenoux, a breeder of dahlias. Desprez sold for a hundred francs the ownership of this rose Cochet, who marketed the rose in 1842.

'Baronne Prévost' is an early representative of the first state of development of the Hybrid Perpetual class. Hybrid Perpetuals emerged in the 1830s, a complex product of marrying Chinas, Portlands, Bourbons, and Noisettes. At first Hybrid Perpetuals competed with the Bourbons, but soon became very popular as an exhibition rose.

DESCRIPTION

Known for its beauty, hardiness, and general versatility, 'Baronne Prévost' has been available in America since 1848. Thick clusters of globular buds open flat and quartered, with as many as 100 petals, in a deep rose pink. A small button eye dots the center. The large, very fragrant blooms are 3½ to 4 inches across. Free-flowering, 'Baronne Prévost,' provides a mass of color.

Vigorous and erect, with growth up to 5 feet tall and about 4 feet wide, these bushy plants have dark green, somewhat coarse leaves, and thick, thorny canes.

Fertilize generously for an abundance of blooms. During dormancy, prune down approximately one half their height to keep plants compact and to ensure continuous blooms. Tolerant of poor soils, disease resistant, and winter hardy, 'Baronne Prévost' can be spotted growing wild in the countryside.

BLOOM TIME: Mid to late June with good repeat through summer and early fall.

USES: Beautiful in an informal border or good as a specimen plant near a house or along pathways. Suitable for hedging.

POSITION: Sun.

ZONES: 4 to 9.

'Baroness Rothschild'

TYPE: Hybrid Perpetual

PARENTAGE: Sport (mutation or genetically altered branch) of
'Souvenir de la Reine d'Angleterre'

INTRODUCED: 1868 by Pére, France

 HISTORY

Originally discovered by Pernet Pére, this rose is also known as 'Baronne Adolphe de Rothschild' or 'Mme. La Baronne de Rothschild.'

Hybrid Perpetuals, a group of roses that originated in the 1830s, were the forerunners of the Hybrid Teas. The first to flower perpetually, or re-currently, Hybrid Perpetuals are the result of a union of many roses. The old-fashioned 'Baroness Rothschild' is also thought to be closely related to the Portland rose, a rose type that originated in the late 1800s from a cross between a Damask and a Gallica.

DESCRIPTION

'Baroness Rothschild' produces some of the most beautiful flowers of the old roses. The perfectly formed, large, double flowers are a soft, clear pink. The cup-shaped blooms, 5½ to 6 inches wide, are dense with pink petals on the outside, growing deeper pink towards the center. One of the largest blooms of old roses, the larger outer petals surround many tightly packed, shorter central petals. Lightly fragrant, the flowers generally appear singly, but very free-flowering, on erect stems. 'Baroness Rothschild' grows 4 to 6 feet tall and spreads about 3 to 4 feet. The bush is thick with medium gray-green, semiglossy leaves with large leaflets. The canes are smooth with few thorns. 'Baroness Rothschild' is disease resistant, tolerant of poor soils, and winter hardy.

BLOOM TIME: Mid to late June with fair repeat in fall.

USES: Because the flowers appear singly and are held on erect, strong stems, 'Baroness Rothschild' makes an excellent rose for cutting. It also does very well in containers and is fine for hedges, bedding, or massed in groups.

POSITION: Sun.

ZONES: 4 to 9.

'Belle de Crécy'

TYPE: Gallica

PARENTAGE: Unknown

INTRODUCED: 1848 by Roeser, France

 HISTORY

Grown before 1848—some rose historians have placed this rose between 1830 and 1836—the 'Belle de Crécy' was grown and introduced to the market by the Frenchman Roeser of Crécy en Brie. It's not clear whether the rose is named for Madame de Pompadour, who is said to have favored it in her garden at Crécy, or if the rose is simply named for Roeser's hometown.

Among the many rosy-mauve and purple Gallicas available, 'Belle de Crécy' is one of the most reliable and free-flowering. The flowers go through a succession of shades of violets, purples, mauves, and pinks. Buds are pink and open into a deep pinkish-purple, maturing to violet-mauve, eventually turning to lavender-gray. Blooms open wide, flat, and quartered, with reflexing (curved back) petals around a green button eye. The 2½- to 3-inch wide flowers may have as many as 200 petals. This exquisitely fragrant rose blooms for about three weeks in mid-summer. Reaching about 4 feet tall with a 3-foot spread, the plant's growth is rounded and compact. Foliage is medium to dark green with dull, rough leaves. The canes are nearly thornless. 'Belle de Crécy' is tolerant of poor soils, disease resistant, and winter hardy, although it is somewhat susceptible to mildew in wet weather.

BLOOM TIME: Mid-June with no repeat.

USES: In formal and informal rose collections, 'Belle de Crécy' contrasts nicely with white roses. Its compact size also makes it a fine rose for containers and suitable for low hedges.

POSITION: Sun.

ZONES: 4 to 9.

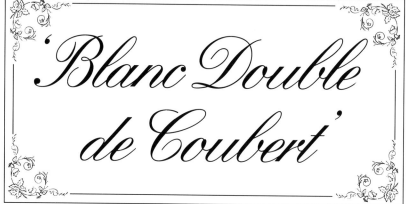

TYPE: Rugosa
PARENTAGE: *R. rugosa* x 'Sombreuil'
INTRODUCED: 1892 by Cochet-Cochet, France

HISTORY

Pierre Cochet and his two sons Philémon and Scipion, were rosarians from Suisnes, France, who bred and introduced many roses in the 1800s.

Rugosa roses are native to China, Japan, and Korea. They have two unique qualities: they are very hardy and they are almost alone among wild roses that repeat bloom. Crossing a Rugosa rose with the beautiful Tea rose 'Sombreuil' resulted in this new rose with the loveliest qualities of its parent plants.

One of the most beautiful of white roses, 'Blanc Double de Coubert' also has the most intoxicating of fragrances. The large, snowy-white flowers are perfectly formed, 3 to 4 inches across, with loosely arranged petals around a yellow center. Buds appear with a hint of blush color, open in a semi-double form, and flower with remarkable consistency. Foliage is rich green and bushy, with leathery leaves that turn bright yellow in the fall. Shrubs are moderately vigorous, growing 4 to 6 feet tall, with a spread of about 4 to 5 feet. Bright orange-scarlet hips appear after flowering.

Deadheading will encourage more blooms. To groom and keep hips, cut only the spent petals. Prune only for thinning and to remove old, dead wood, or to shape.

One of the best performing Rugosas, 'Blanc Double de Coubert' is extremely resistant to disease, tolerant of poor soils and shade, and extremely hardy.

BLOOM TIME: Early to mid June with good repeat bloom throughout summer.

USES: Excellent in an informal bed or as a hedge, 'Blanc Double de Coubert' has a delicious fragrance, making it desirable near pathways or sitting areas. Because of its vigor, it makes a valuable plant for stabilizing steep banks or a fine planting at the seashore.

POSITION: Sun or part shade.

ZONES: 3 to 8, occasionally 2.

'Charles de Mills'

TYPE: Gallica

PARENTAGE: Unknown

INTRODUCED: 19th Century

 HISTORY

Neither the parentage nor the origination date of the 'Charles de Mills' rose is known. One old rose source suggests that the breeder was Desportes, a Frenchman active between 1800 and 1835 and author of *Rosetum Gallicum*, published in 1828. Despite its misty origins, 'Charles de Mills' is one of the few old roses listed in the top ten most popular U. S. roses at the 1991 World Federation of Roses.

'Charles de Mills' is a spectacular, dark magenta rose known to bloom in shades from crimson to purple and violet. Flowers are extra large, up to 4½ inches across, fully double, and well quartered with about 200 petals. Blooms first open a rich rosy-purple but gradually darken in a succession of crimson tones. The flower is a unique shape, its extremely full petals forming a flat cup, as if the petals have been sheared across the top in an elegant, even way. When fully open, the bloom shows a green cavity rather than a button eye at its center. This moderately perfumed rose is immensely free-flowering, smothering the bush in blooms for as many as six weeks. Growth is upright and vigorous, reaching 4½ to 5 feet tall, with very dark, rough, green leaves. Canes are moderately bristly with sparse thorns. Disease resistant and winder hardy, tolerant of poor soils—but especially productive in rich soil—'Charles de Mills' is one of the finest performers among the old roses.

BLOOM TIME: Mid to late June, no repeat bloom.

USES: Good in general garden purposes, but deserving of a prominent position in a rose garden. 'Charles de Mills' spreads considerably, making a good hedge. It also makes a wonderful boutonniere. Plants are easy to root from cuttings.

POSITION: Sun.

ZONES: 4 to 9.

'Fatin-Latour'

TYPE: Centifolia

PARENTAGE: Unknown

INTRODUCED: 19th century

 HISTORY

Nothing is known of the date or the origin of 'Fatin-Latour.' Found in an old English garden sometime in the mid to late 1800s, the owner had labeled the rose the "Best Garden Rose." Classified as a Centifolia because its bloom and habit are characteristic of the type, it also has some China rose qualities. It was named for the great French painter, Henri Fantin-Latour, whose finest paintings always included the old roses, many of which may be the rose named for him.

A glorious Centifolia, 'Fatin-Latour' makes a beautiful garden shrub. Dark rosy-pink buds open to a delicate, pale blush-pink color, each one about 3 1/2 inches wide. Forming a circular cup shape, the petals are a slightly darker pink in the center, later opening flat and growing paler. The fully double, sometimes quartered flowers have outer petals that reflex (curve back) with maturity to expose a small button center. Blossoms have a light, sweet fragrance. The multitude of flowers bloom in clusters of 2 to 5, which stay open a long time. Very free-flowering, 'Fatin-Latour' makes a large, rounded bush, 5 feet tall with a 4-foot spread. The dark green, rounded leaves have 3 to 5 large leaflets and canes with few thorns. 'Fatin-Latour' will tolerate poor soils.

BLOOM TIME: Mid to late June, no repeat bloom.

USES: Makes a beautiful cut flower, or grow it in small groups or in a shrub border. 'Fatin-Latour' is suitable for informal or woodland plantings and makes a fine hedge.

POSITION: Sun.

ZONES: 4 to 9.

'Félicité Parmentier'

TYPE: Alba
PARENTAGE: Unknown
INTRODUCED: Before 1828

 HISTORY

Known since classical times, Alba roses were widely grown during the Middle Ages and appear in many paintings of that period. They are thought to be the result of natural hybridization between the Dog rose (*Rosa canina*) and either the Damask rose or *Rosa gallica*.

Parentage of 'Félicité Parmentier' is unknown but *R. damascena* may possibly be related. Both of these roses are characterized by openness of their branches.

'Félicité Parmentier' is a stunning rose that develops rounded, creamy-yellow buds in late spring and early summer before opening to soft pink. Blooms consist of a multitude of petals formed into a tightly-packed cluster, wonderfully-scented and perfectly quartered. They open fully to form a small, round shape about 2½ to 3 inches across. Flowers later reflex (curve backward) and fade to cream at the edges. Blooms open somewhat slowly and last long on the stems. Growth is bushy but compact, only 4 feet high by 3 feet wide, with light green leaves and contrasting dark thorns. Minimum pruning is necessary, but wait until second or third year because best blooms grow on second-year wood. Occasional hard pruning will encourage more blooms. 'Félicité Parmentier' is tolerant of poor soils, but in dry seasons in sandy soil, the flowers sometimes fail to open properly.

BLOOM TIME: Mid to late June with fair repeat bloom.

USES: An extremely fragrant rose, it is excellent for cutting, lasting a long time in water. Its small and compact size makes it a good choice for small gardens. It is also suitable for woodland or country settings and makes a fine small hedge.

POSITION: Sun or part shade.

ZONES: 3 to 9.

'Frau Karl Druschki'

TYPE: Hybrid Perpetual
PARENTAGE: 'Merveille de Lyon' x 'Mme. Caroline Testout'
INTRODUCED: 1901 by Lambert, Germany

 HISTORY

The 'Frau Karl Druschki' rose was raised by Peter Lambert who, in 1900, entered it in the German National Rose Society's competition for the best new German rose. The winner was to be named 'Otto von Bismarck.' Because its pure white petals were deemed unsuitable to represent the Iron Chancellor, Lambert's rose won second place and so he named the rose instead for the wife of the president of the Rose Society. Enthusiastically received, 'White American Beauty' (the name given to the rose in America) was described as the "most popular rose in America" in a 1920s rose catalog.

This beautiful, pure white rose was called 'Snow Queen' in England and 'White American Beauty' in the United States; nurserymen thought 'Frau Karl Druschki' was difficult to remember and, during World War I, feared the rose by its other name would fall victim to anti-German sentiment. The large, double flowers, 4 to 4½ inches wide, bloom abundantly in large clusters. The thick, rose-pink buds are pointed, and open to pure white flowers with high centers, like Hybrid Teas. When fully extended, the petals form a cup shape. This rose has little or no fragrance. A vigorous shrub, it can reach 5 to 7 feet tall, more if trained as a climber. Its habit is upright and thick with soft, medium green leaves; the nearly smooth canes have few thorns. To keep the plant in a woody bush form, prune it back hard each year, as you would a Hybrid Tea. Although not generally thought of as a climber, its vigorous and arching canes make it an excellent rose for pillars and fences. To encourage climbing, prune minimally, opening the center and training the canes laterally to induce growth to 8 to 12 feet. Remove old wood annually in late winter or early spring. Although disease resistant, it can be somewhat susceptible to black spot. It is one of the most weather-resistant white roses and is winter hardy.

BLOOM TIME: Mid to late June with good repeat throughout the summer and into the fall.

USES: Plant several bushes together to best effect. Makes an excellent thick hedge. Arching canes make it ideal for the back of the border or for use as a climber.

POSITION: Sun.

ZONES: 4 to 9.

'Harison's Yellow'

(Rosa x harisonii)

TYPE: Species

PARENTAGE: Unknown, probably *R. foetida persiana* x *R. pimpinellifolia*

INTRODUCED: 1830 by Harison, United States

 HISTORY

Often referred to as the "Yellow Rose of Texas," 'Harison's Yellow' was actually the first rose raised by a New Yorker in the center of New York City. George Harison, a Manhattan attorney, is credited with the first artificially hybridized rose in America. (Often debated, opponents think Harison's rose occurred as a chance seedling.) Despite its urban roots, 'Harison's Yellow' was the rose most commonly planted by Western pioneers. The Oregon Trail is marked by clumps all along the way, and evidence of the plant is recorded in every state west of the Mississippi.

DESCRIPTION

'Harison's Yellow' might well be called the All-American rose. Planted prodigiously by settlers all over the West since the mid-1800s, this vigorous, healthy rose is still widely grown.

Nicely shaped and doubled, the small, very bright yellow flowers are 2 to 2½ inches across, each with about 20 to 25 petals. Numerous small buds open in a globular form, but flatten as they mature, often to show a cluster of darker yellow stamens at the center. The fragrance is delicate and the plants are extremely free flowering. 'Harison's Yellow' makes a glorious display for weeks and provides vivid color in the border before most other old-fashioned roses bloom.

A vigorous shrub, usually 6 to 8 feet, the plant can form a large mass over the years, and grow to over 10 feet high and 12 feet wide. The rich foliage is grayish-green, with stems bristling with needle-like thorns. The canes are long and arching. Tolerant of poor soils and shade, it is resilient and winter hardy. Once rooted, it is unaffected by drought and cold. Often thriving on neglect, the plant needs only to be thinned every few years to prevent it from becoming too dense.

BLOOM TIME: Mid May to early June with no repeat.

USES: 'Harison's Yellow' is excellent in an informal shrub border or as a hedge. The rose can also be used to climb fences, walls, or other supports. Suckers are easily rooted.

POSITION: Sun or part shade.

ZONES: 3 to 9.

'Jacques Cartier'

(Syn. 'Marquise Boccella')

TYPE: Portland

PARENTAGE: Unknown

INTRODUCED: 1868 by Moreau-Robert, France

HISTORY

Often seen listed as 'Marquise Boccella' in North America, 'Jacques Cartier' was named after the famous sixteenth century French navigator and explorer, who discovered the St. Lawrence River in North America. The rose is a fine example of the Portland roses, which were raised in the mid-1800s, and originated from the 'Duchess of Portland' rose, named after the English Duchess who reportedly brought the rose to England from Italy.

DESCRIPTION

A classic old rose beauty, 'Jacques Cartier' is known for its compact growth, rich scent, and perpetual flowering habit.

Flowers are large, 3½ to 4 inches across, and come in a clear, rich pink. Full, fat, rosy-pink buds open into shapely full-petaled flowers, the outer petals slightly reflexing (curving back) to expose prominent button eyes. Blooms fade to a paler pink and become quartered and flat with maturity, displaying that traditional old rose form. Held erect on short stems and blooming in clusters of three, the flowers have a wonderful perfume. Growth is compact with an erect habit, generally about 3½ to 4 feet tall and 3 feet wide. The dense, handsome foliage is light green. Leaves have 5 to 7 leaflets. Canes are short with numerous thorns.

'Jacques Cartier' is tolerant of poor soils and shade, and is winter hardy.

BLOOM TIME: Mid June with good repeat, often continuous bloom.

USES: A beautiful cut flower, 'Jacques Cartier' is excellent for small gardens because it is both compact as well as perpetual-flowering. Suitable for planting in groups, edging, or as a low hedge, this versatile rose also does fine grown in containers.

POSITION: Sun or part shade.

ZONES: 6 to 9.

TYPE: Polyantha

PARENTAGE: 'Étoile de Mai' x 'Marie Pavie'

INTRODUCED: 1901 by Lambert, Germany

HISTORY

Polyanthas were a group of roses introduced around the turn of the century. The French started the new group, but only a few had been introduced until Peter Lambert of Germany took an interest in them. 'Katharina Zeimet' (also known as 'White Baby Rambler') was one of the first and best of all the Polyanthas to make its way to the marketplace. Polyanthas fell from favor after the 1940s, but have recently seen a renewed—and richly deserved—interest.

'Katharina Zeimet,' like its parent 'Marie Pavie,' is one of the finest old Polyantha roses. The delicacy of the flowers is seldom found in the small rose varieties. The small buds are a distinctive rosy-pink, but open into fully double, pure white flowers. The blooms are small, about 1½ to 2 inches across, but are produced continuously in large clusters all through the season. When fully opened, the many loose petals show a dark green, almost black center. The fragrance is light and sweet. A compact, low-growing bush reaches 2 feet with a 2-foot spread. The dark greeen, glossy foliage is dense and plentiful all season. A strong and tough little plant, 'Katharina Zeimet' tolerates poor soils, is disease resistant, and winter hardy. Occasional black spot may appear late in the season and flowers may fade to brown in severe heat.

BLOOM TIME: June with continuous repeat through the fall.

USES: An excellent rose for massing together as edging in a border or along a walk or as a hedge, 'Katharina Zeimet' works well among other shubs. Its width also makes it suitable for a ground cover. It is also a fine container plant and perfect in small gardens.

POSITION: Sun.

ZONES: 4 to 9.

'Könige von Dänemark'

(Queen of Denmark)

TYPE: Alba

PARENTAGE: 'Maiden's Blush' seedling

INTRODUCED: 1826 by Booth, Denmark

 HISTORY

In 1816, John Booth raised a seedling from 'Maiden's Blush,' a rose cultivated before 1600, and originally called it 'New Maidenblush.' Distribution was limited through 1821. Upon developing enough good stock, Booth entered the rose in his nursery catalog for 1826 under the name 'Könige von Dänemark,' after obtaining permission from the king to name it after the queen.

DESCRIPTION

'Königen von Dänemark' is one of the most elegant of the old roses. Its individual blooms are perfectly formed in a vivid rose-pink, often described as carmine-pink, which turns to a softer, paler pink with age. Buds are cup-shaped at first, but the multitude of nearly 200 petals open into a full, perfectly quartered bloom. The petals curve back slightly to expose a small button eye at the center. Fully expanded, the blooms reach 3½ inches across and are wonderfully fragrant. A medium-sized shrub of about 4 or 5 feet, it occasionally reaches 6 feet, with a 4-foot spread. The rose's habit is somewhat slender and open, with foliage of blue-green, rough leaves, and very thorny canes. Like all Albas, it is easy to grow, performing even in poor soils and some shade. But 'Königen von Dänemark' will reward good cultivation with exquisite blooms. Resistant to black spot, mildew, and rust, the plant is winter hardy.

BLOOM TIME: Early to mid June, no repeat bloom.

USES: 'Königen von Dänemark' makes a beautiful cut rose and does well in containers. It can be grown as a small climber on a wall or other support. It is also suitable for hedging or for woodland planting. Cuttings are fairly easy to root.

POSITION: Sun or part shade.

ZONES: 3 to 9.

'La Reine Victoria'

TYPE: Bourbon

PARENTAGE: Unknown

INTRODUCED: 1872 by Schwartz, France

 HISTORY

Bourbon roses appeared around 1820, about the same time as Noisette roses. They were named for Bourbon Island (now known as Réunion Island) in the southern Indian Ocean.

Among the most popular Bourbon roses of the Victorian era, 'La Reine Victoria' and her sport (a mutation or genetically altered branch) 'Madame Pierre Oger' were called Victorian shell roses because of their thin, delicate, shell-like petals.

DESCRIPTION

A longtime favorite and true old rose classic, 'La Reine Victoria' produces beautiful, rich lilac-pink flowers of a silky texture, with overlapping petals, darker on the outer edges, paler at the base. The cupped-shaped blooms are full and very rounded, and retain their form through maturity. The very fragrant flowers grow up to 3½ inches wide, semi-double to almost double, and repeat pro-fusely. Slender shrubs grow about 4 to 5 feet tall, but only 3 feet wide. Leaves are a soft, dull, medium green, with smooth canes and few thorns.

For best results, cultivate 'La Reine Victoria' in rich, fertile soil with good air circulation to fend off black spot. Disease resistant and winter hardy, this rose is often seen listed simply as 'Reine Victoria.'

BLOOM TIME: Mid to late June with good repeat bloom in the fall.

USES: An exquisite cut flower, 'La Reine Victoria' bears flowers on long, erect stems. This rose works well in both formal and informal gardens and is excellent in containers. With hard pruning, it makes a fine rose for a small garden.

POSITION: Sun.

ZONES: 5 to 9.

'Louise Odier'

TYPE: Bourbon

PARENTAGE: Unknown

INTRODUCED: 1851 by Margottin, France

 HISTORY

The original Bourbon rose was found on the French island of Bourbon in 1817 by the Parisian botanist Bréon. Seeds of this rose were sent to Paris to Jacques, the gardener to King Louis Philippe, who began to raise new roses from the seeds. The result was a new group, the French Bourbon roses, commonly called Bourbon roses today.

These roses, dating before the 1920s, are often defined as "antique roses."

DESCRIPTION

A superb and vigorous Bourbon, 'Louise Odier' produces camellia-like, perfectly shaped flowers in warm pink, shaded softly with lilac. The very full blossoms are double, sometimes quartered, and can grow up to 3½ inches across. Buds open first into a cup shape, then open flat around the edges. Neatly rounded, half-open petals form a circular center. Graham Stuart Thomas, English horticulturist, rosarian, and author, calls this rose "a bourbon with the old-world perfection of shape." The richly-perfumed blooms are free-flowering and borne in dense clusters, which sometimes produce an arching effect due to the weight of the blooms. Plants grow 5 to 6 feet tall, with a width of about 4 feet. Slender, upright, and bushy growth with attractive light to medium green leaves grow along smooth canes with few thorns. 'Louise Odier' is tolerant of shade, disease resistant, and winter hardy. Keep the soil well worked and well fertilized for good autumn flowering.

BLOOM TIME: Mid to late June with good repeat bloom throughout the summer.

USES: The shape and perfume make 'Louise Odier' a lovely cut flower for bouquets. Use it in formal or informal beds or combine it with 'La Reine Victoria' and 'Madame Pierre Oger.' This rose can also be trained on a low trellis or used as a hedge.

POSITION: Sun or part shade.

ZONES: 5 to 9.

'Madame Hardy'

TYPE: Damask

PARENTAGE: Unknown

INTRODUCED: 1832 by Hardy, France

 HISTORY

Julien Alexandre Hardy, the curator of the Luxembourg Gardens in Paris, dedicated this rose to his wife. Although Hardy raised thousands of seedlings, 'Madame Hardy' is the one for which he is most remembered. The parentage is uncertain; the rose is a cross between a Damask and possibly a China or Bourbon, but seems to have some *Rosa centifolia* characteristics as well. Still popular today, 'Madame Hardy' was voted one of the top ten all-time favorites at the 1991 meeting of the World Federation of Roses.

DESCRIPTION

Truly one of the most beautiful of the old garden roses, 'Madame Hardy' has few peers. The pure, snow-white flowers have a delicious fragrance, with blooms free-flowering in dense clusters. Just a hint of blush-pink is evident as the flowers unfold, but this quickly fades into the purest white. Opening first into a cup-shape, then becoming flat, with the outer petals lightly reflexing (curving back), the flower's central petals are quartered around a small green eye. Flowers are 3 to 3 1/2 inches across, very full, and double, with as many as 200 petals.

Extremely vigorous, plants grow to 5 to 6 feet tall with a 5-foot spread. Upright and bushy, they can be grown as a dense shrub or contained on a pillar or fence. Although rarely used as a climber, 'Madame Hardy' is easily trained on a low support. New growth leaves are pale green, turning to a medium green with maturity. Stems are upright and canes are moderately thorny. 'Madame Hardy' is disease free and winter hardy, and can withstand cold climates. It is also tolerant of shade and poor soils.

BLOOM TIME: Mid May to mid June with no repeat.

USES: For best effect, grow in groups of several bushes to provide support and mass of color. A single specimen is lovely on a pillar. 'Madame Hardy' is suitable for hedging, or grow it on a low fence or spread out along a wall. The bloom clusters make beautiful cut flowers.

POSITION: Sun or part shade.

ZONES: 4 to 9.

'*Madame Isaac Pereire*'

TYPE: Bourbon

PARENTAGE: Unknown

INTRODUCED: 1881 by Garcon, France

 HISTORY

Little is known of 'Madame Isaac Pereire.' Old rose history suggests that it may be a seedling of *R. borboniana*.

The name, more than likely, honors a wife of one of the Pereire brothers, who were financiers and bankers during the Second Empire, when Louis Bonaparte (Napoleon III) was on the throne.

Best known for its intense perfume, 'Madame Isaac Pereire' may perhaps be the most fragrant of all roses. A typical Bourbon, it has very large flowers, up to 5 inches across, in a rich, warm pink shaded with crimson. The globular blossoms are double and very full, cupped at first and quartered on opening; the outer petals roll back at the edges. A group of yellow stamens are exposed in the center when fully opened. Flowers are produced in clusters and have an unforgettable perfume. A recurrent bloomer, 'Madame Isaac Pereire' flowers particularly well in autumn.

It is a very vigorous shrub, usually reaching 5 to 7 feet, but known to climb to 10 feet. This height, along with shoots that can reach up to 6 feet in a season, make the rose a valued climber as well as a shrub. Foliage is bushy, with dark green, semiglossy leaves and moderately thorny canes.

This rose will endure poor soil, but performs best with rich, fertile soil, especially if grown as a climber. It tolerates some shade, is disease resistant and winter hardy.

BLOOM TIME: Mid to late June with fair repeat bloom.

USES: 'Madame Isaac Pereire' works well in informal rose gardens, shrub borders, or used as a climber on adequate support, such as pillars or walls.

POSITION: Sun or light shade.

ZONES: 5 to 9.

'Old Blush'

TYPE: China
PARENTAGE: Unknown
INTRODUCED: 1752 by Parsons, Sweden

HISTORY

Also known as 'Parson's Pink China' rose, 'Old Blush' was discovered in China by a physician on a Swedish ship, who brought a specimen back to his friend, the botanist Carolus Linnaeus, in Upsala. If seventeenth-century paintings serve as historical records, this rose bloomed in China for at least a century before being brought to Sweden.

The common rose of American dooryards in the 1800s, 'Old Blush' is the rose that was growing at the Appomattox Courthouse when General Robert E. Lee surrendered to General Ulysses S. Grant. It continues to grow there today.

Perhaps the most beloved of the China roses is 'Old Blush.' An attractive bush with dainty, rosy-pink flowers in small clusters, each flower is 3 inches wide, double in form, with 25 to 30 petals. Long, pointed, deep rose-colored buds open into a loosely-cupped formation in pure pink, with a warmer rose-pink in the center. Blossoms darken with age, creating several shades of pink, rose, and pale cerise. The flowers have little or no fragrance. A perpetual bloomer, 'Old Blush' begins blooming early and finishes late. For this reason it was once called the "Monthly Rose." Growth is upright and moderately vigorous, reaching 4 to 5 feet tall. If grown as a small climber, it can reach 6 to 8 feet. The shrub is bushy, with long, smooth leaves in a glossy, medium green. Canes are smooth, with few thorns. Young shoots are a reddish-brown color. Orange hips appear in the fall. Little, if any, pruning is necessary; remove only dead wood.

Plants are disease resistant, tolerant of shade and poor soils, and drought resistant. Many have thrived over a hundred years on nothing more than neglect. This rose is fairly hardy, needing winter protection in colder climates. In warmer climates, such as those in Texas and California, they are evergreen.

BLOOM TIME: All season bloom.

USES: 'Old Blush' can be grown to good effect in a group, formal rose bed, or in a mixed border. It can be grown as a small climber, performing beautifully on pillars and posts. It will perfom in northern climates, but may not thrive as beautifully as it does in southern latitudes.

POSITION: Sun or part shade.

ZONES: 7 to 9.

'Paul Neyron'

TYPE: Hybrid Perpetual

PARENTAGE: 'Victor Verdier' x 'Anna de Diesbach'

INTRODUCED: 1869 by Levet, France

 HISTORY

Antoine Levet of Lyons, France, developed this rose in 1869. He named it for his friend Paul Neyron, although it was a tragic tribute, as Mr. Neyron was killed the following year in the Franco-Prussian War.

A Hybrid Perpetual, 'Paul Neyron' is a cross between two roses other types in the same class, 'Victor Verdier' x 'Anna de Diesbach', and a descendant of the beautiful 'La Reine.' Enthusiastically received, the rose became so popular that "Neyron pink" entered the language of color and fashion.

❧ DESCRIPTION ❧

'Paul Neyron' has one of the largest flowers of all roses. Its peony-like blooms reach 4 to 5 inches in diameter, but can be as wide as 6 or 7 inches. Roses bloom in a deep rose-pink shade with a lavender tint, somewhat lighter on the back. The double blooms are tightly packed with 65 to 75 petals. Globular in shape, often quartered when fully open, and with a light fragrance, 'Paul Neyron' is extremely free-flowering, producing a mass of un-fading blooms for several weeks. A vigorous shrub, it grows upright to 5 or 6 feet with a spread of 3 to 4 feet. Long, solid stems are arching and produce large, glossy, dark green leaves. Canes are relatively smooth with few thorns. Sturdy, beautiful, disease resistant, winter hardy, and tolerant of poor soils, 'Paul Neyron' is a good selection for ease of cultivation with sensational results.

BLOOM TIME: Mid to late June and fair repeat in the fall.

USES: Makes an exquisite, large cut flower, a lovely specimen shrub, or an effective group planting. It also works well as a bedding plant or a hedge. A fine rose for growing in containers, 'Paul Neyron' is suitable for forcing or growing under glass.

POSITION: Sun.

ZONES: 4 to 9.

'Reine des Violettes'

(Queen of the Violets)

TYPE: Hybrid Perpetual

PARENTAGE: 'Pius IX' seedling

INTRODUCED: 1860 by Millet-Malet, France

 HISTORY

Although classified as a Hybrid Perpetual, 'Reine des Violettes' could very well be grouped among the Bourbons, its characteristics are so similar in growth and bloom. The bloom is often compared to a Gallica as well.

Raised in France, 'Reine des Violettes' has been on the market continually since 1860.

🙦 DESCRIPTION 🙤

Possibly the very best of the Hybrid Perpetuals, 'Reine des Violettes' is a healthy, robust shrub with stunning blooms. Often called the bluest rose, it is known for the deep violet-purple flowers. Blooms are 3 to 4 inches across in a full-petaled, rosette formation with up to 75 petals that open flat and quartered around a button eye. The velvety violet color becomes paler towards the center, and the petals curve inward to form a wide, flat bloom. The petals disperse rather quickly upon reaching perfec-tion, but repeat blooms continue reliably through the summer. Blooms are rich with fragrance. Growth is upright, reaching 5 to 6 feet tall and 3 to 4 feet wide. Sparse gray-green foliage grows on thick, erect branches. The canes have very few thorns.

Although tolerant of poor soils, for best performance plant in rich, well-drained soil with lots of sun and out of the wind; neglected plants will be short-lived.

BLOOM TIME: Mid to late June, repeat bloomer throughout the summer and early fall.

USES: An excellent choice for growing in containers, 'Reine des Violettes' also makes a fine hedge as well as a beautiful specimen rose in formal beds.

POSITION: Sun.

ZONES: 4 to 9.

Rosa x centifolia

(Cabbage Rose, Rose of Provence)

TYPE: Centifolia

PARENTAGE: Unknown

INTRODUCED: Before 1600

HISTORY

Thought to be one of the very oldest roses. *R. x centifolia* (hundred-petaled rose) was described for the first time by Clusius (Charles de l'Ecluse) in *Rariorum Historia* in 1601. There is also a hundred-leaved rose known to exist as early as 300 B.C. The old herbalists called *R. x centifolia* the "Queen of Roses." Often listed as a species, it is probably a complex hybrid of four species, *R. gallica*, *R. phoenicia*, *R. moschata*, and *R. canina*. Centifolia is widely portrayed in paintings by the Old Dutch masters, and *R. x centifolia* is the rose from which the Centifolia group takes its name.

Surely one of the most beautiful roses, *R. x centifolia* has been a favorite for hundreds of years. Large flowers of exquisite shape bloom a deep, rich pink that darkens toward the center. Cupped, almost ball-shaped, and fully doubled, the flowers consist of a hundred or more petals and have the most intoxicating of old rose perfumes. The heavy, nodding blooms are fully quartered when open and bloom singly and in clusters. A medium-sized shrub, semi-vigorous in growth, generally reaching about 5 to 6 feet with a spread of 5 feet, the plant supports large, rounded, drooping leaves, coarsely toothed in gray-green. The branches are prickly, with abundant hooked thorns. New shoots up to 4 or 5 feet long appear each summer, which need to be trimmed back about halfway. The open habit and loose shoots sometimes need the support of stakes or close planting.

R. x centifolia tolerates poor soil, but thrives with good cultivation. It flowers best in warm dry weather, and is susceptible to mildew in wet climates or continued wet weather.

BLOOMTIME: Mid June to early July with no repeat.

USES: *R. x centifolia* is a must in an old rose collection or an informal garden. It makes a beautiful cut flower and can be grown as a hedging if supported properly.

POSITION: Sun or light shade.

ZONES: 4 to 9.

'Rosa Mundi'

R. gallica 'Versicolor'
R. gallica 'Rosa Mundi'

TYPE: Gallica

PARENTAGE: A sport (mutation or genetically altered branch) of *R. gallica officinalis*

INTRODUCED: 1500s or before

HISTORY

The legendary striped rose, *R. gallica 'versicolor'* is best known as 'Rosa Mundi.' Mentioned in texts since 1581, it was known to be in cultivation before the sixteenth century. It is generally thought that returning Crusaders introduced the rose into England, as its parent is indigenous to the Middle East. The name 'Rosa Mundi' comes from the romantic legend of King Henry II and his mistress Fair Rosamond. Should the legend be true, the rose would have been familiar in Europe since the twelfth century. 'Rosa Mundi' is so widely grown, it is sometimes called the "Rose of the World. "

DESCRIPTION

The most beautiful and best known of the striped roses, 'Rosa Mundi' never fails to attract attention with its brilliant crimson and pale pink stripes—and no two blooms are exactly alike. Blooms are fairly large, 3 to 3 1/2 inches across, semi-double, and quite fragrant. The buds are rather thick and open somewhat flat around a central cluster of yellow stamens. A massive amount of flowers blooms upright above the foliage, creating a stunning display that lasts well. Round, red hips appear late in the season. Semi-vigorous in growth, 'Rosa Mundi' reaches 4 feet high and about 3 to 4 feet wide, forming a rounded, compact bush. Leaves are medium to dark green and rough. Canes have few thorns. 'Rosa Mundi' will tolerate even the poorest soils and shade and is winter hardy. Although disease resistant, plants are prone to mildew without good air circulation. Compost annually and prune old wood from the base of the bush. In early spring, prune and shorten branches.

BLOOM TIME: Mid to late June with no repeat bloom.

USES: One of the best roses for a low hedge or a mixed border, 'Rosa Mundi' makes an excellent cutting flower, and the hips also provide ornamental value in the border or in arrangements. Low-growing, it can be used as a ground cover or thicket in difficult positions or in poor soil, or can be used as a screen or a barrier. It also does well in containers and can be trained—with work—as a standard.

POSITION: Sun or part shade.

ZONES: 4 to 9.

'Rose du Roi'

TYPE: Portland

PARENTAGE: Unknown

INTRODUCED: 1815 by Lelieur, France

 HISTORY

Discovered by Écoffay, a gardener to the florist Souchet in Sévres, France, 'Rose du Roi' was raised from seed in 1815. The Comte Lelieur, former director of the French Royal Gardens, propagated it and Souchet brought it to market. A sensation in its day, 'Rose du Roi' was the first perpetual blooming rose created and marketed. The original name was 'Comte Lelieur,' but it was renamed 'Rose du Roi' (Rose of the King) because of Louis XVIII's fondness for it. Also classified as a Hybrid Perpetual, the rose is sometimes listed as 'Lee's Crimson Perpetual.'

DESCRIPTION

The deep magenta coloring and the perpetual flowering make 'Rose du Roi' an appropriate plant in the finest rose gardens. Graceful, stunning flowers are 2½ inches wide and bloom in a loose, double formation of 100 or more petals. The perfectly formed flowers are a vivid magenta with hues of violet throughout. Outer petals are somewhat large, with shorter, tighter ones in the center. Flowers are held upright and usually solitary, blooming consistently through fall. When fully opened, the blooms are highly scented. Growth is vigorous and compact, reaching 3 feet tall and 3 feet wide. A short, rather spreading bush with medium green foliage, 'Rose du Roi' has semiglossy leaves and moderately thorny canes. The branches are light green with some reddish tints in places. Prune back about one third of the canes after first bloom for best repeat. Plants are tolerant of some shade and poor soils, disease resistant, and winter hardy, although less vigorous in colder climates.

BLOOM TIME: Mid to late June with good repeat bloom.

USES: A superb cut flower, 'Rose du Roi' provides a nicely scented bouquet. It also makes a fine hedge, and is suitable for growing in containers.

POSITION: Sun or light shade.

ZONES: 6 to 9.

'Safrano'

TYPE: Tea
PARENTAGE: Unknown
INTRODUCED: 1839 by Beauregard, France

HISTORY

Thought to be from 'Parks Yellow' x 'Madame Desprez,' 'Safrano' was raised by Beauregard at Angers, France. 'Parks Yellow' Tea rose provides the glowing yellow color to the blooms of this exquisite Tea rose.

Tea roses came about in the early 1830s from roses shipped from China that were often crated with tea. Bred from these roses not long after their arrival, 'Safrano' is often called Europe's first Tea rose.

'Safrano' is often cited as a favorite among expert rose growers and hybridists. Its flowers are an unusual creamy yellow-apricot color with copper shading toward the center. The bright yellow, almost orange buds are pointed, and open into flat, fully double flowers with high centers. The color of the petals pales with age. The fragrance is mild but sweet. Free-flowering blooms provide a constant display through first frost. 'Safrano' reaches about 3 to 4 feet, with a narrow spread of 2 to 3 feet. The attractive foliage has a purple-bronze color on new growth, and turns to dark green over time. Plentiful leaves have five leaflets. 'Safrano' has smooth branches and few thorns. Plants perform best in sunny positions. 'Safrano' is one of the oldest of the Tea roses and worth seeking out.

BLOOM TIME: Mid June with continous repeat bloom.

USES: Grow 'Safrano' in groups for best effect. It performs well in containers and can be forced or grown in a green house.

POSITION: Sun.

ZONES: 7 to 9.

'Salet'

TYPE: Moss

PARENTAGE: Unknown

INTRODUCED: 1854 by Lacharme, France

HISTORY

Grown by Francois Lacharme of Lyons, France, who raised a variety of *R. centifolia muscosa*. Moss roses are sports (mutations or genetically-altered branches) of Centifolias and Damasks. Their flower stalks, lobes, and even their hips are covered with a growth that resembles moss.

'Salet' is the most reliable repeat bloomer of all the Moss roses. Its charming, rosy-pink blooms are 2½ to 3 inches wide, with 60 to 70 petals. The perfectly shaped, pink buds open into full, double, globular blooms, which flatten and are slightly quartered. When fully opened, the outer petals reflex (curve backward) and fade as the flower ages. The blooms are nicely scented, often described as having a musk fragrance, which is more pronounced in the evening. There is only a modest quantity of reddish-brown moss on the sepals and stalks. The flowers bloom in a slightly deeper color in autumn. Blooms are supported by a medium-sized, upright shrub reaching 4 to 5 feet with a 3-foot spread. The stems are arching, with bright green new-growth leaves that turn to a dull, medium green with age. The canes are quite thorny. Tolerant of poor soils and disease resistant, 'Salet' was cited as one of the best winter-hardy roses in a 1991 report of the Old Garden Rose Committee of the American Rose Society.

BLOOM TIME: Mid to late June with fair repeat in the fall, reliable repeat in the South.

USES: Especially useful for the smaller garden, 'Salet' can be grown in containers, is suitable for hedging, and makes a fine cut flower.

POSITION: Sun.

ZONES: 4 to 9.

'Sir Thomas Lipton'

TYPE: Rugosa

PARENTAGE: *R. rugosa* 'Alba' x 'Clothilde Soupert'

INTRODUCED: 1900 by Van Fleet, United States

HISTORY

Dr. Walter Van Fleet, one of America's foremost rose breeders, was a physician in New York who gave up medicine to practice horticulture. Working at the Department of Agriculture, he developed many new plants, but was known primarily for his roses. Specializing in "dooryard" roses," he also created the climbing 'American Pillar' (see p. 66), the rose for which he is most reknown. 'Sir Thomas Lipton' is a rugged Rugosa he raised in 1900. It was introduced to the market by Conard and Jones, the nursery establishment that was responsible for marketing Van Fleet's roses.

'Sir Thomas Lipton' is a Rugosa rose and, like others in this category, will grow almost anywhere with minimal care and provide a generous supply of flowers. Blooms are a creamy white, semi-double to fully double in a cupped shape. Thick, pale buds open into loosely formed flowers with the outer edges of petals reflexing (curving back) slightly. Blooms sometimes resemble small peonies. Flowers are 2 to 3 inches across and have an exceptional clove-scented fragrance. Borne singly or in clusters, flowers bloom continuously from early summer though fall. A vigorous and bushy plant, 'Sir Thomas Lipton' grows 4 to 5 feet tall and about 4 feet wide, sometimes growing larger in warmer climates. The dark green, leathery foliage provides a nice autumn color. Canes are green with lots of thorns. Rugged, yet trouble free, 'Sir Thomas Lipton,' like all Rugosas, is hardy and grows under difficult conditions, even extreme, such as ocean spray and salt winds. Plants are disease resistant, long-lived, and tolerate shade and poor soils, even sand and clay.

BLOOM TIME: Early June, with good repeat throughout the season.

USES: 'Sir Thomas Lipton' makes an excellent thick hedge, often inpenetrable. It is suitable for growing in containers, and works well in mass plantings for large areas, including as a windbreak from the seashore.

POSITION: Sun or part shade.

ZONES: 3 to 8, occasionally 2.

'Souvenir de la Malmaison'

TYPE: Bourbon

PARENTAGE: 'Madame Desprez' x unknown Tea

INTRODUCED: 1843 by Beluze, France

HISTORY

'Souvenir de la Malmaison' was named in re-membrance of Empress Josephine's famous garden at Malmaison, where she created the world's most complete collection of roses. The seeds were first sown in 1840 by Jean Beluze, a rose breeder from Lyon. Beluze knew he had a special rose and carefully guarded his stock until he made it available in the Lyon market in 1843 for twenty-five francs a shrub. A climbing sport was discovered by Bennett, a British rosarian, in 1893. The rose is sometimes listed as 'Queen of Beauty and Grace.'

60

'Souvenir de la Malmaison' is the most beautiful and popular of the old roses. The flowers are a soft blush-pink with a rich tint of cream, and lightly lilac when opened. Each bloom is beautifully proportioned, cup-shaped at first and fully double, later becoming flat and distinctly quartered to form a large and beautiful flower about 4 to 5 inches across. The outer petals are large, with smaller ones squeezed together in the middle like rumpled satin. The petal coloring becomes more creamy pale with age. The gracefully nodding blooms are borne singly and provide a delicious, spicy perfume.

Robust and vigorous, shrubs grow 5 to 6 feet high with a similar spread. The bushy foliage has a reddish tint with new growth, then turns to medium green. The leaves are deeply serrated and canes are moderately thorny. Prune by shortening the strong shoots by one-third, weak shoots by two-thirds.

Good cultivation is essential to establish this rose. It performs less well in wet weather, sometimes not opening properly in these conditions. Provide good circulation to avoid midlew. A climbing form reaches 12 feet or more, but does not repeat as well.

BLOOM TIME: Early to mid June with reliable repeat.

USES: This rose deserves a special place in the formal or informal rose garden. It is suitable for containers. Its long stems and perfumed flowers make it magnificent for cutting and bouquets.

POSITION: Sun.

ZONES: 5 to 9.

'Stanwell Perpetual'

(R. pimpinellifolia 'Stanwell Perpetual')

TYPE: Species, Hybrid *pimpinellifolia* (Scotch rose)

PARENTAGE: *R. x damascena bifera* ('Autumn Damask') x *R. pimpinellifolia*

INTRODUCED: 1838 by Lee, England

 HISTORY

'Stanwell Perpetual' occurred as a chance seedling in a garden at Stanwell, Essex, England. It is thought to have originated as a natural hybrid between *R. pimpinellifolia* and a perpetual-flowering pink Damask, probably *Rosa damascena bifera*. It was brought to the market by the nurseryman John Lee of Hammersmith, England, in 1838.

This superb old variety seems to make everyone's favorite list, and for good reason. 'Stanwell Perpetual' has the toughness and hardiness of the Scotch rose and the wonderful ability of 'Autumn Damask' to flower throughout the season. It has deliciously scented light pink flowers, 3 to 3½ inches across, which fade to a blush-white with age. A cluster of yellow stamens form in the center. The blooms are abundant, fully-doubled, with as many as 50 petals in a loose, somewhat informal formation. The small leaves are a deep blue-green with up to 9 leaflets. The canes have lots of thorns.

'Stanwell Perpetual' is a vigorous grower, reaching 5 feet or more with a spread of 5 feet. Prune out weaker growth after flowering or during the winter. For tidiness, a severe pruning should be done every few years, taking out older growth altogether.

'Stanwell Perpetual' is tolerant of poor soils and shade and, when well established, is disease resistant and winter hardy. It is the only Scotch rose hybrid that is a reliable repeat bloomer.

BLOOM TIME: Early to mid June with reliable repeat.

USES: Use 'Stanwell Perpetual' in rose collections, borders, or in informal country settings, or grow them as shrub or pillar roses. Suitable for growing in pots, 'Stanwell Perpetual' also can be grown as a hedge; plant several specimens close to one another to provide support.

POSITION: Sun or part shade.

ZONES: 3 to 9.

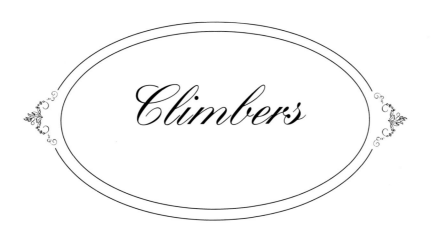

Climbers

'American Pillar'

TYPE: Rambler

PARENTAGE: (*R. wichuraiana* x *R. setigera*) x a red Hybrid Perpetual

INTRODUCED: 1902 by Van Fleet, United States

HISTORY

'American Pillar' was developed by Dr. Walter Van Fleet, one of America's foremost plant breeders, known especially for his climbing roses. First raised at his home garden in New Jersey, it was displayed at the Du Pont estate, now known as Longwood Gardens, and later introduced for sale by the firm of Conard and Jones. It was once one of the most popular roses in America.

DESCRIPTION

A particularly showy plant, 'American Pillar' deserves to regain the popularity it once had. Flowers are vibrant carmine-pink with white central eyes and prominently displayed yellow stamens in the center. Blooms consist of single flowers with 5 petals, 2 to 3 inches wide, with little or no fragrance. Blossoms occur in very abundant, tight clusters for at least four weeks. Red hips appear later in the fall and are quickly enjoyed by birds. Leaves are medium green, glossy, and large. Foliage turns reddish-brown in the fall, making 'American Pillar' an interesting plant throughout the season.

A strong, rampant grower, plants reach 15 to 20 feet tall. Thick, sturdy canes can be easily trained. Prune older canes, keeping the new ones; blooms are produced on second year growth. Remove older wood during the summer to make room for new growth.

'American Pillar' tolerates partial shade and poor soils, but not dry weather; it is subject to mildew when conditions are too dry. Otherwise, it is disease resistant and winter hardy.

BLOOM TIME: Early to mid June, blooming for a long period, usually four weeks or more. No repeat bloom.

USES: Still popular in Europe, 'American Pillar' is often seen as a dramatic rose tunnel in many of the best rose gardens. Grow over pergolas, arches, trellises, high fences, chains, or as weeping standards. Also suitable for growing up into trees. Despite the name, the canes are often too heavy for pillars.

POSITION: Sun or part shade.

ZONES: 5 to 9.

'Cécile Brunner,' Climbing

TYPE: Climbing Polyantha

PARENTAGE: 'Cecile Brunner' sport

INTRODUCED: 1894 by Hosp, United States

HISTORY

The original shrub form of 'Cécile Brunner' was bred by Ducher in 1881, and was named for the daughter of a family of Swiss nurserymen. The climbing form is a sport (a mutation of the parent) discovered in the United States by F. P. Hosp. 'Cécile Brunner' is often called the "Sweetheart Rose" because of the delicate-looking tiny buds and small, shell-pink flowers. At one time it was famous as a buttonhole rose.

The rose known as 'Climbing Bloomfield Abundance' is really 'Climbing Cécile Brunner.'

A little charmer, 'Cécile Brunner' has delicate, silvery-pink blooms that absolutely envelop a pergola or wall with hundreds of flowers. The tapered and pointed buds are elegantly formed into a perfect shape. 'Cécile Brunner' blooms in clusters, each flower only 1 to 1½ inches across, and looks like a miniature Hybrid Tea rose. The pale pink color darkens slightly in the center and has a light, but distinct fragrance. An exceptionally fine and vigorous climber, 'Cécile Brunner' achieves 25 feet of rampant growth in a single season with a spread of 20 feet. 'Cécile Brunner' boasts dense, dark green foliage with small, semiglossy leaves. Canes are smooth with a few thorns, making it easy to work with on supports. 'Cécile Brunner' is tolerant of shade, disease resistant, long-lived, and will grow in most soils. A very reliable climber, it is not winter hardy in severe winter climates.

BLOOM TIME: Mid to late June with good repeat bloom.

USES: The vigorous growth of 'Cécile Brunner' is perfect for walls, pergolas, posts, or the sides of houses. Ideal for growing into trees or over unsightly buildings, it will do fine in a north position, but will not produce an abundance of blooms. It can be forced or grown under glass.

POSITION: Sun or part shade.

ZONES: 4 to 9.

'Dorothy Perkins'

TYPE: Rambler

PARENTAGE: *Rosa wichuraiana* x 'Mme. Gabriel Luizet'

INTRODUCED: 1901 by Jackson & Perkins, United States

 HISTORY

Developed by E. Alvin Miller, a breeder for the firm of Jackson & Perkins, this first successful rambler is named for the granddaughter of the founder of the company. Prior to this rose, no generous-blooming climber would thrive in northern climates, so Jackson & Perkins scored an early winner in 1901 with 'Dorothy Perkins' and it became one of the most popular roses in the country. In fact, it became so popular that it was overplanted and lost favor. Only recently has it begun a comeback.

DESCRIPTION

'Dorothy Perkins' has been famous since its inception. This popular rambler bears colorful cascades of bright pink flowers. Individual flowers are rather small—less than 1 inch wide—and double in form, with about 40 to 45 petals. The bright pink flowers have a somewhat bluish tint and bloom in large clusters, sometimes lasting for six weeks. The fragrance is light. A typical rambler, growth is quite vigorous, reaching 10 to 15 feet in one season, with long shoots. Spread can be up to 8 feet. The dark green leaves are small and glossy, with moder- ately thorny canes. New growth is pliable and easy to train to most corners, turns, or shapes. Prune hard the first season, down to about 4 inches. Flowers bloom the second season. This plant thrives in all types of soil, even the sandy soil of the seashore. It is disease resistant, but susceptible to mildew. Do not plant 'Dorothy Perkins' against a wall or building; good air circulation is needed to avoid mildew. A tough old rose, 'Dorothy Perkins' is found in old abandoned areas, often thriving on neglect.

BLOOM TIME: Late June to mid-July, occasionally repeats bloom in fall, usually in warmer areas.

USES: A quick grower, 'Dorothy Perkins' has long canes that can be wrapped around arches, pergolas, fences, lattices, porches, doors and windows. It can also be used in a trailing form to cover a bank or to cascade down a hillside, or used as a wide-growing ground cover.

POSITION: Sun or part shade.

ZONES: 4 to 9.

'Gloire de Dijon'

TYPE: Climbing Tea
PARENTAGE: 'Souvenir de la Malmaison' x unknown Tea
INTRODUCED: 1853 by Jacotot, France

 HISTORY

Raised by Jacotot of Dijon, France, 'Gloire de Dijon' was exhibited in June 1852 at the Société d'Horticulture de la Cote d'Or at Dijon and awarded first prize. The judges at this meeting were so impressed with this rose they gave it the name 'Gloire de Dijon' (The Glory of Dijon). The following year, 'Gloire de Dijon' received the gold medal at the Paris Exhibition. This famous old climbing rose, once found in many gardens around the country, was often known as 'Old Glory.'

The striking coloration, handsome foliage, and wonderful scent has made 'Gloire de Dijon' popular for over a hundred years. The rose blooms in a lovely and unusual creamy yellow color with shades of pink, apricot, and peach, shaded darker in the center. The flowers are very large and full, 4 to 4½ inches wide, and have about 50 to 60 petals. The doubled, occasionally quartered, blooms have a globular shape that opens flat with larger petals at the outer edge and smaller petals toward the center. The fragrance is a delicious tea scent. An abundance of flowers bloom continuously until frost. Thick, heavy foliage displays medium green, glossy leaves with arching branches that reach 10 to 12 feet. Stems are reddish when young, with smooth, moderately thorny canes. Pruning should be minimal, just enough to remove old and dead wood. The flowering period is extended by bending down the shoots. This rose performs best in dry, warm weather; in wet weather it is prone to black spot. Otherwise, 'Gloire de Dijon' is disease resistant, will tolerate light shade, but is not winter hardy.

BLOOM TIME: Early June with good repeat bloom.

USES: A superb variety for wall or pillar, 'Gloire de Dijon' is flexible enough for shaping into chains and garlands. The warm color of this rose works especially well against dark brick walls. It is suitable for forcing or for growing in a greenhouse.

POSITION: Sun or light shade.

ZONES: 5 to 9.

'Madame Alfred Carriere'

TYPE: Climbing Noisette

PARENTAGE: Unknown

INTRODUCED: 1879 by Schwartz, France

HISTORY

'Madame Alfred Carriere' was developed by Joseph Schwartz of Lyons, France, who introduced sixty-three of his own varieties. (Another fifty-seven were marketed by his widow.) Noisette roses, which originated in Charleston, South Carolina, became quite popular in Europe and were a favorite of Gertrude Jekyll, the famous English gardener and writer, and Vita Sackville-West, whose 'Madame Alfred Carriere' roses are seen on the wall at Sissinghurst Castle.

'Madame Alfred Carriere' is one of the best white climbers. It makes a lovely display against an old wall or grown over a pergola. The large, cupped blooms are creamy white with tints of soft pink. The flowers are double, 2½ to 3 inches wide, with about 35 petals, and have a moderate Tea rose fragrance. Abundantly flowering, 'Madame Alfred Carriere' gives a magnificent display over a long period. The foliage is lush, with light green, semi-glossy leaves on stiff stems. Growth is vigorous, reaching 10 to 15 feet tall, with moderately thorny canes. Easy to train over arches, pergolas, or arbors, 'Madame Alfred Carriere' is tolerant of shade and does well on a north wall. Disease resistant but only semi-hardy, it needs winter protection. Gertrude Jekyll recommended training the rose as a hedge along wires supported by posts; this arrangement makes gathering the flowers easier.

BLOOM TIME: Mid to late June, excellent repeat bloom, almost continuous.

USES: A lovely and fragrant flower for cutting, 'Madame Alfred Carriere' makes a delightful bouquet. It may be most beautiful on a wall or alongside a house, but it can be trained over most sturdy supports, or growing up into trees. If placed on top of a retaining wall, its branches will hang down freely. This rose is also suitable for forcing or growing under glass.

POSITION: Sun or part shade.

ZONES: 5 to 9.

'*Paul Ricaut*'

TYPE: Bourbon hybrid

PARENTAGE: Unknown

INTRODUCED: 1845 by Portemer, France

HISTORY

Portemer of Gentilly, France, originated 'Paul Ricaut'—a hybrid of a Bourbon and a Centifolia—in France around 1837, but the rose was not introduced until 1845. It is not known who the rose is named for, but Sir Paul Ricaut, an English diplomat, is frequently mentioned.

Often categorized as a Centifolia, or Cabbage rose, because of the multitude of petals, 'Paul Ricaut' is recorded in the oldest rose literature records as a Bourbon.

One of the most free-flowering of the old-fashioned roses, 'Paul Ricaut' has very large pink flowers, up to 4 inches across. The many-petaled blooms are distinctively quartered, open flat, and hang gracefully from the stem. Dark scarlet buds open into deep pink, very fragrant flowers, which are densely packed along long, arching stems. The foliage is large, very dark green, with coarse, stiff leaves. Thorns are on the back of the petiole, or leaf stalk. 'Paul Ricaut' has a vigorous growth habit, easily reaching 6 to 8 feet in one season with a width of about 4 feet. Although 'Paul Ricaut' can be used as a hedge with no support, it is most beautiful on a pillar or high fence or other kind of support. Train young canes around supports; older canes become stiff and are more difficult to work with. 'Paul Ricaut' requires very little care, other than occasional light pruning for shape or to remove dead wood. An extremely hardy rose with little disease problems, this rose often thrives on neglect.

BLOOM TIME: Early to mid June, blooming for at least a month, with good repeat.

USES: Easy to train on a pillar, post, or along a fence, 'Paul Ricaut' also makes a fine hedge, growing about 5 feet high with no support.

POSITION: Sun.

ZONES: 5 to 9.

'Sombreuil, Climbing'

TYPE: Tea

PARENTAGE: Unknown

INTRODUCED: 1850 by Robert, France

HISTORY

'Climbing Sombreuil' was introduced in 1850 by Robert of Angers, France, who took over the nursery previously owned by another famous rose breeder, J. P. Vibert. The only thing known of its parentage is that it was a seedling from a Hybrid Perpetual called 'Gigantesque.' Some of the oldest rose literature lists this rose as 'Mademoiselle de Sombreuil,' named for Marie-Maurille Virot de Sombreuil, a young woman who, during the French Revolution, saved her father from the September massacres.

One of the best climbing Tea roses, 'Climbing Sombreuil' has beautiful creamy white flowers with a trace of pink at their center. Yellowish buds are pointed and open into flat, double flowers, each quartered with a button-eye center. Perfectly formed blooms are large, 3 to 4 inches across, usually in clusters, and sweetly scented. The leaves are dense, with dark green, glossy foliage. The rosarian and author Peter Beales described 'Climbing Sombreuil' in his book *Roses*, as "flowers [which] have numerous petals, and open to form flat rosettes that can only be described as the most perfect of Old Roses." A hardy, vigorous grower, it grows to 12 feet wide and 8 feet high and blooms until first frost. Stunning on a wall, lattice, fence, or growing on a pergola, 'Climbing Sombreuil' is easy to train, and will bloom during the first season. It grows in sun, but flowers last longer in partial shade. This rose needs very little pruning—only to remove old or dead wood. It is also winter hardy.

BLOOM TIME: Mid June with repeat in autumn.

USES: 'Climbing Sombreuil' grows on walls, lattices, fences, arches, or pergolas. It makes a lovely cut flower, and is suitable for forcing or growing under glass.

POSITION: Sun or part shade.

ZONES: 7 to 9.

'Zéphirine Drouhin'

TYPE: Bourbon

PARENTAGE: Unknown

INTRODUCED: 1873 by Bizot, France

 HISTORY

According to some sources, 'Zéphirine Drouhin' was found wild in Turkey. It was known to be growing in Europe in 1868, the date sometimes recorded as its introduction. In 1873 it was officially introduced in France by Bizot, a rose grower from Dijon. Bizot named it for Madame Zéphirine Drouhin, the wife of an amateur horticulturist in Semur, France. It was often called by other names, including 'Charles Bonnet' in Switzerland and 'Madame Gustave Bonnet' in England. Although popular all over Europe, it did not become popular in the United States until the 1930s.

DESCRIPTION

A beautiful, thornless rose, 'Zéphirine Drouhin' is a quintessential old-fashioned rose that has been the most popular of the Bourbon roses for many years. Its semi-double, vivid rose-pink blooms are white at the base. Its many loose petals are richly-scented. The blooms fade to a creamy pink as they age. The leaves are very attractive, with a coppery-red color when first appearing and turning to a rich gray-green. The shoots and canes are also a coppery-bronze color and remain so throughout the season. The plant grows to 10 to 15 feet in height, and about 6 feet wide. The flowering season can be long, and may bloom all summer in the right conditions, especially in warm climates.

'Zéphirine Drouhin' is a vigorous grower. Its long, arching canes are easy to work with because they have no thorns; they are easily wound around and over most any support. When first planted, prune hard to encourage new growth. 'Zéphirine Drouhin' will not bloom the first season, and possibly not for 2 or 3 seasons. Do not prune again until well established, then remove only dead wood.

Give this rose plenty of air circulation to avoid mildew and blackspot. 'Zéphirine Drouhin' is tolerant of poor soils and shade.

BLOOM TIME: Mid June. In warm area, it blooms again after the heat of autumn.
Under perfect conditions, it can bloom throughout the season.

USES: Because it has no thorns, 'Zéphirine Drouhin' is ideal planted near a house or alongside a pathway. Beautiful around most any broad support, including arches, windows, lattices, fences, pillars, or up into trees. It is also excellent for cutting, making wonderfully perfumed bouquets, and it is a spectacular shrub in a mixed border.

POSITION: Sun.

ZONES: 5 to 9.

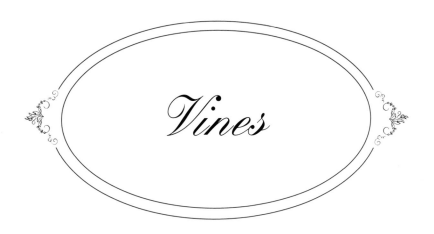

Vines

Black-Eyed Susan Vine

Clockvine

Thunbergia alata

HISTORY

Native to central and south Africa, Madagascar, and Asia, but now common throughout the tropics through garden escapes, Black-Eyed Susan vine was first introduced into England in 1823 from Zanzibar, and later brought to the Americas. The genus *Thunbergia* was named for Dr. Carl Peter Thunberg (1743-1828), a young botanist who was sent by Carolus Linnaeus to various parts of the world, especially Asia, to collect plants. Later he be-

came a professor of botany at Uppsala University in Sweden, and a successor to Linnaeus. Despite its common name, Black-Eyed Susan vine, but for the color of its blooms, does not resemble the daisy of the same name so common on the prairies. Clockvine, another common name, describes how the vine, which twists to look like a clock hand turning. The species *alata* is Latin for winged, and refers to the winged leaf stems.

DESCRIPTION

A perennial climber, usually grown as an annual, Black-Eyed Susan vine grows up to 10 to 15 feet in a season, quickly covering porches, arbors, spilling down walls, steep banks, or hanging from pots. Cheery yellow flowers grow about 1½ inches across from a purple tube, and develop five petals surrounding a dark, almost black center. Blooms are yellow-orange or creamy white. The foliage is heart-shaped (like ivy) and is light green. The twining stems easily grip trellises. If you choose to grow it on a smooth surface, such as a wall or post, provide something for it to cling to. The plant blooms from July through October, but if started early, Black-Eyed Susan vine will bloom all summer. Easily grown in containers, the vine can be brought in for winter and makes an excellent houseplant.

CULTIVATION

Sow seeds outdoors after last frost or start indoors 6 to 8 weeks ahead. Plant in rich, moist, well-drained soil. Provide a warm, sunny position, sheltered from the wind. Water generously and regularly during the growing period. Feed with a liquid fertilizer twice monthly from June to August. Little, if any, pruning is needed. If grown as a houseplant, give it lots of light with a warm, humid temperature and adequate support. It may be taken outside again in spring.

COMMENTS: *T. grandiflora*, sky flower, grows to 10 feet and has showy, sky-blue flowers. An excellent plant for warm climates, but not hardy in the North.

POSITION: Sun or light shade.

PROPAGATION: Seed or cuttings.

Canary Bird Vine

Canary Creeper, Canary Nasturtium
Tropaeolum peregrinum (syn. *T. canariensis*)

HISTORY

Native to Peru and Ecuador, the familiar Canary Bird vine was found early in the eighteenth century by the French naturalist Feuilée growing near the town of Lima in Peru. Although the flower is canary yellow, the plant is named instead for the Canary Islands, where it was introduced on its way from South America to France. The Spaniards in the Canary Islands named it *paxarito*, little bird plant, because the blooming plant resembles the flight of hummingbirds.

In 1755, Canary Bird vine was introduced to England, where its particularly dainty blooms became the prizes of cottage gardens. It is not known whether the plant came to North America from England or from South America.

DESCRIPTION

A graceful and elegant annual climber, Canary Bird vine has lemon-yellow flowers, each about 1 inch long. The three lower petals are narrow and fringed at the tips. The two upper petals are also fringed, but larger and with red spots. The green spur is curved and protrudes slightly from the flower. Pale blue-green leaves are deeply cut into five finger-like sections on smooth stems. The blooms are numerous, and appear from July through September, and blooms from September through winter in warm areas. Canary Bird vine is a rapid climber, running up to a height of 6 to 12 feet in a single season. The plant requires only a minimum of support, such as wires or strings, but do not use thick supports, suc as trellises. The plant readily covers arbors, fences, and walls.

CULTIVATION

Canary Bird vine needs little care and often thrives in the poorest of soils. Sow outdoors after all danger of frost. Seeds may be started indoors, but seedlings do not transplant well. Ideal soil is light and not too rich; too much fertilizer produces more leaves and fewer flowers. Space 8 to 12 inches apart and do not overwater; water only when soil is dry. Provide support as soon as growth begins. Although it prefers sun, Canary Bird vine will grow in partial shade. Grow away from other, more vigorous climbers that could easily overgrow and suffocate this plant.

COMMENTS: *T. speciosum*, the perennial climbing flame creeper, has spectacular, red-orange flowers, but is rather difficult to establish in gardens.

POSITION: Sun or part shade.

PROPAGATION: Seed or cuttings.

Clematis

Clematis species

HISTORY

The ancient Romans cultivated clematis on the walls of their houses, not only for its beautiful flowers, but also because they believed it served as protection against thunderstorms. In German lore, the opposite held true. Germans thought the plant attracted lightning and thunderbolts.

Clematis was grown before 1569 by Hugh Morgan, the pharmacist to Queen Elizabeth I. It was dubbed Lady's or Virgin's Bower as a compliment to the queen.

By the mid 1800s, it became so fashionable to grow clematis that entire gardens were planted only in clematis in its various forms and colors. In 1862, *Clematis* x *jackmanii*, bred by the reknowned British clematis breeder George Jackman, became, and continues today to be, one of the most popular and widely grown varieties. By 1597, European varieties of clematis had reached the Americas. It was used extensively by Native Americans. The fibers were made into rope, the leaves and flowers were used for horse medicine, and the delicate seed-carrying styles were used for tinder. Clematis was also grown by Thomas Jefferson at Monticello.

The name *Clematis* is derived from the Greek *klema*, meaning vine or twig. Common names included traveller's joy, greybeard, grandfather's whiskers, father time, and hedge feathers. The early American settlers called clematis old maid's bonnet because of the sheen of the dark blue flowers.

DESCRIPTION

Clematis is often referred to as "Queen of the Climbers" and deservedly so. It comes in almost every color, produces lavish flowers, and, by selecting different varieties, blooms can be enjoyed from early spring through autumn. Clematis comprises an extensive group, the most popular and readily available being: Large-flowering clematis, usually *C. patens* or *C. langinosa*, which offers the greatest variety of hybrids in nearly every color, and blooms from June to August. *C. x jackmanii*, one of the most beautiful in form and color, with large, violet-purple flowers up to 5 inches across that bloom abundantly all summer. *C. montana*, a spring bloomer with a profusion of pure white flowers 1 to 1½ inches across, with a strong vanilla fragrance. *C. terniflora* (often listed *as C. paniculata*), or autumn clematis, the one to grow for fragrance in September and October, with white flowers 1 inch wide, and masses of ornamental silver seedheads following the flowers. (This variety is a rampant climber, suitable to areas of long hot summers and falls). *C. virginiana*, another fall-flowering species with off-white, 1¼ inch blooms that produces a mass of flowers over vigorous growth, and looks especially stunning among the golds and browns of autumn. *C. crispa*, known as the marsh or curly clematis, one of the small-flowering varieties with urn-shaped, blue flowers that bloom from July to September.

CULTIVATION

Purchase plants for easiest method; seed germination takes at least four weeks and the hybrids do not come true to seed. Clematis needs rich soil with lots of organic matter. Set the collar of the plant at least 2 to 3 inches below the soil surface. The base and roots of the plant should be in shade and the top of the plant should be in sun or partial shade. Mulch the base; the roots should be kept cool and moist at all times. Fertilize twice a month during the growing season. Provide trellis, wire netting, iron railing or other support of metal, wood, or plastic onto which they can climb.

The species that bloom on old wood, including *C. montana*, *C. lanuginosa*, and *C. patens*, should be pruned only after flowering, with pruning limited to thinning. Others that flower on new growth should be pruned at the end of winter to encourage new shoots. Cuttings can be taken in June-July.

POSITION: Sun or part shade.

PROPAGATION: Seed or cuttings.

Clematis 'Madame Eduard André' (left). Autumn Clematis (right). Clematis 'Dr. Ruppel' (opposite).

Crossvine

Trumpet Flower Vine

Bignonia capreolata

HISTORY

Native to eastern North America, crossvine grows from Virginia west to central Illinois, and south to Florida and Louisiana. The plant was first taken to Europe around 1700, where cultivation began. The common name comes from the unusual characteristic of the stem; when cut crosswise, the parts of the stem form a cross.

In 1700, French horticulturist and plant breeder J. P. de Tournefort named the genus in honor of Abbé Jean Paul Bignon (1662-1743), the court librarian to Louis XV. At this time, the genus was comprised of about fifteen species. By the time Carolus Linnaeus named the plant in 1768, there were only seven species. Over the next two centuries, the numbers increased to more than a hundred, many of which have been reclassified. Unfortunately, the crossvine fell from favor and only *B. capreolata* remains today.

DESCRIPTION

A vividly colored and striking plant, crossvine attaches to virtually any object by means of its branching, self-clinging tendrils. Tubular, funnel-shaped flowers are 2 inches long and bloom in showy clusters. The dark orange-red flowers have yellow interiors, and bloom in abundance in early summer against dark green, long, and pointed foliage. Fruits shaped like 6-inch long pea pods appear in autumn. Growing to 30 feet or more, crossvine makes an excellent wall plant. It can also be grown on the ground in a trailing manner, which looks nice among rocks and boulders.

CULTIVATION

Sow crossvine seed in spring or purchase plants and place in well-drained, fertile soil—even light clay—in a sunny location with plenty of air circulation. Water regularly in summer. Evergreen in mild climates, crossvine needs a sheltered position in northern zones up to about Zone 6.

Prune all weak and dead growth regularly; before the flowering period, shorten the tips of all long growths by 1 to 3 feet. Cuttings should be taken in late spring.

COMMENTS: Crossvine performs well in containers, which restricts the root system to limit abundant foliage and increase flowering.

POSITION: Sun.

PROPAGATION: Seed or cuttings.

Dutchman's Pipe

Pipevine
Aristolochia durior

HISTORY

Native to eastern and central North America, Dutchman's Pipe grows from Pennsylvania and Minnesota south to Georgia. Prior to air conditioning, Dutchman's Pipe was grown on porches and houses all over the country for the dense shade it provided in hot summer months.

In folklore, Dutchman's Pipe is associated with childbirth. Chewing the roots of this plant was said to relieve the pains of labor. According to the me-

dieval *Doctrine of Signatures*, objects that resemble each other are said to be related; because the flower of Dutchman's Pipe looks like a fetus, the plant was linked to the act of childbirth. The old-time common name Birthworts testifies further to this link in lore.

The genus name *Aristolochia* is a combination of two Greek words, *aristos*, meaning "best," and *lochos*, meaning "childbirth."

DESCRIPTION

Dutchman's Pipe, once one of the most popular vines, is making a comeback. Grown for its dense foliage of large, heart-shaped leaves and complement of interesting flowers, Dutchman's Pipe is one of the best vines for screening. The U-shaped flowers resemble a Dutchman's or Meerchaum pipe. The spectacular, odd-shaped flowers are about 1½ inches long, and bloom in a unique yellowish-brown throughout the month of June. Foliage is dense, with leaves growing between 6 to 14 inches long. A tall, high-climbing vine, Dutchman's Pipe grows rapidly and reaches heights of 30 feet and more. The blue swallowtail butterfly, also called the pipe vine swallowtail butterfly, favors this plant as a host for its larvae, which feed on the leaves after they are hatched.

CULTIVATION

Sow seeds directly in the garden after the last frost or place purchased plants in any ordinary, well-drained garden soil. Hardy vines, Dutchman's Pipes are adaptable to most situations, including shade and dry soil; however, it's best to water well in dry weather. Climbers with a twining habit, the plants need support; plant at the base of a pergola, wall, arch, or near a large tree. Give Dutchman's Pipe plenty of room; it grows so quickly it will crowd out other vines growing nearby. In spring, cut back previous season's growth to two or three nodes. Cuttings can be taken in late summer.

POSITION: Sun or partial shade.

PROPAGATION: Seed or cuttings.

Honeysuckle

Lonicera species

HISTORY

It is not known when honeysuckles were first introduced into gardens, but it is known that the British Earl of Lincoln grew them in his garden before 1286. In the 1600s, honeysuckles are known to have been growing in a corner of the orchard of Anne Hathaway's cottage. Shakespeare mentioned them in *Much Ado About Nothing* and again through the character Oberon, in *A Midsummer Night's Dream.* In 1656, the royal gardener John Tradescant brought *L. sempervirens,* a native North American honeysuckle, to England for cultivation. Honeysuckles reached their pinnacle during the nineteenth century in England, when nearly every cottage, arbor, or garden was covered with its spicy, perfumed flowers.

Honeysuckles had several practical uses. The gentlewomen of Elizabethan England kept a conserve of the flowers to help relieve asthma, bronchitis, and cramps. The tightly-coiling trunks of honeysuckle were used to make canes and walking sticks.

The honeysuckle genus is named for Adam Lonicer, a sixteenth century German naturalist. An old-fashioned common name of goat's leaf came from the Latin words for "goat" and "leaf" because it was a favorite food of goats. The Chinese name for this plant means "gold and silver flower."

DESCRIPTION

Deliciously sweet-smelling honeysuckle blooms in tubular or bell-shaped flowers of white, yellow, orange, or red, and are produced in abundance on quick-growing vines. After the blooms fade, red, blue, or black fruits—a favorite food for birds—take their place on the vines. Honeysuckle is semi-evergreen and climbs easily over other vegatation. Nocturnal moths pollinate honeysuckle at night.

L. sempervirens, trumpet or coral honeysuckle (zones 3 to 9), is native to the United States. It is a handsome vine with orange to scarlet trumpet-shaped flowers, but has no scent. It blooms from May to autumn and is the hardiest of all honeysuckle vines. It is evergreen in mild climates.

L. periclymenum, European woodbine honeysuckle (zones 4 to 9), comes in fragrant white, yellow, or crimson flowers, which bloom throughout the summer.

L. x heckrottii, goldflame honeysuckle (zones 5 to 9), is long-blooming in bright coral and yellow, with a slight fragrance at night.

L. japonica, Japanese honeysuckle (zones 4 to 9), blooms in yellow or white from July to October. Delicious, sweetly-scented flowers are small but abundant.

L. j. halliana, Hall's honeysuckle (zones 4 to 9), was introduced before 1860. It has perfumed white flowers which bloom in summer. Vigorous, it is best grown where it can be controlled by annual pruning. It is also excellent for checking erosion.

CULTIVATION

Extremely easy to cultivate, honeysuckles flourish almost anywhere, but, for best results, use a loamy, well-drained soil, that stays moist. Purchase plants or start seeds indoors in March. When seedlings are large enough to handle, put them in a single pot to encourage root growth. Place plants 24 to 28 inches apart in the garden in spring. Prune young plants to encourage branching and to control size. Water adequately; honeysuckles do not do well in droughts. Prune in winter or spring before plants leaf out. Regular pruning of old plants is unnecessary except for tidiness. Honeysuckles need wires or trellises for support.

POSITION: Sun or part shade.
PROPAGATION: Seed or cuttings.

Hydrangea, Climbing

Hydrangea anomala petiolaris

HISTORY

The first hydrangea (*H. arborescens*) was first introduced to Europe from North America in 1736 and by 1823 was a common sight on terraces and window boxes on both continents. But enthusiasm for hydrangeas did not come until the late 1800s with the introduction of the Asiatic species, whose various types were raised as houseplants and exhibited in competitions. Native to China and Japan, the climbing hydrangea, became a beautiful and regular feature on the walls of cottages and manor houses alike, and later on the claps and field-stones of American homes.

Native Americans used the dried hydrangea roots to prepare diaphoretic, cathartic, and diuretic remedies. In Japan, the stems of some forms of hydrangea were used for making walking sticks, pipes, and umbrella shafts. The bark was used to make paper.

DESCRIPTION

A summer-flowering vine of great beauty, climbing hydrangea is completely different from other species of hydrangea. This hardy, vigorous, deciduous climber clings readily to walls, columns, or tree trunks in the same manner as ivy, with aerial roots. Leaves are heart-shaped, 2 to 5 inches long, and form a glossy, green, dense cover over the surface to which it is attached. The creamy white blooms form large, flat heads, 6 to 8 inches wide. This lace cap type of flower consists of small fertile flowers surrounded by a few larger sterile flowers. Climbing hydrangea blooms in midsummer from about mid June to July, and grows to reach heights of 30 feet or more.

CULTIVATION

Characterized botanically as a shrub, hydrangea is easiest to grow from purchased plants, which are more readily available than seed. Prepare cool, rich, well-drained, moderately acid soil; however, most ordinary garden soil is adequate. Unlike some hydrangeas, climbing hydrangea flower color is not influenced by the soil and always remains a creamy white. Water frequently to keep the soil moist. Prune lightly; flowers bloom on previous year's branches. Climbing hydrangea is an excellent choice for smooth surfaces of stone, masonry and wood in your garden or along your house walls.

COMMENTS: Climbing hydrangea is very similar to and often confused with *Schizophragma hydrangeoides*, which is not as ornamental.

POSITION: Sun or part shade.

PROPAGATION: Seed or cuttings.

Ipomoea

Morning Glory Vine, *Ipomoea purpurea*
Moonflower, *Ipomoea alba* (formerly *Calonyction aculeatum*)
Cardinal Climber, *Ipomoea tricolor* (formerly *Quamoclit coccinia*)
Cypress Vine, *Ipomoea quamoclit* (formerly *Quamoclit pennata*)

HISTORY

Native to tropical America and introduced to Asia from Mexico around 1840, the Japanese have raised the cultivation of Ipomoeas to a fine art. Grown in pots with extremely careful training, raising these plants has been a highly fashionable art in Japanese horticulture since the 1830s, when a single seed of a rare variety could cost more than ten or fifteen dollars.

The genus name *Ipomoea* is derived from the Greek *ips*, meaning vine tendril, and *homoios*, meaning similar, and describes the plant's habit of climbing by means of its tendrils, like a vine.

The original genus name for moonflower was *Calonyction* and is Greek for night beauty, which aptly describes this beautiful plant.

The former genus name for cypress vine and cardinal climber was *Quamoclit*, from the Greek meaning dwarf bean.

The *Ipomoea* genus includes a diverse group of plants, many of which number among the most popular flowering annual vines. Several were classified botanically under separate genuses until recently. Among the easiest and most available are morning glory vine, moonflower, cypress vine and cardinal climber. All bloom from midsummer to frost.

Morning glory vine is an annual with 3-inch pink, purple, white, or blue flowers . The hairy stems produce heart-shaped leaves, about 4 to 5 inches long. Stems grow rapidly to about 10 feet, clambering over fences or posts, or even along the ground.

Moonflower has pure white, funnel-shaped flowers that are deliciously fragrant. Blooms are large, 5 to 6 inches across, and open in early evening and close around noon the following day. The heart-shaped leaves are large and dark, providing a contrasting backgound for the stunning flowers. A vigorous climber that grows 10 to 15 feet, moonflower is a perennial in frost-free climates, and otherwise is grown as an annual. Plant near porches or windows to take advantage of the lovely perfume.

The cardinal climber is a perennial grown as an annual that flowers the first year. It has a striking, scarlet-red flower, about 2 to 3 inches long with a white throat. Its leaves are deeply lobed and dark. It was recently categorized with *I. tricolor*, which includes *Ipomoeas* mostly of blue and purple—one of the most beautiful being the variety 'Heavenly Blue.'

Cypress vine is an annual that grows 20 to 25 feet, with deep crimson, elongated, funnel-shaped flowers about 1½ to 2 inches long. The leaves are markedly different from the other Ipomoeas, resembling finely divided cypress needles.

CULTIVATION

These four vines are best started by seed and sown directly in the garden. Nick or file the seed coat opposite the seed scar and soak overnight to speed germination. Seeds can be started about six weeks ahead, but are difficult to transplant, so start in peat pots to minimize shock. Plant in warm soil. To prolong the bloom season, sow successively every two weeks through June. Space 8 to 12 inches apart in average, or even poor soil. Ipomoeas will flower more if not fertilized. They self-sow easily. These vines climb by tendrils and need the support of trellises or fences.

POSITION: Sun or light shade.
PROPAGATION: Seed or cuttings.

Moonflower (right). Cypress vine (left). Morning glory vine (opposite).

Passion Flower

Passiflora caerulea

HISTORY

In the early 1600s, a Spanish missionary returned from Mexico and described a miraculous flower, one that contained within itself the Savior's Cross and the symbols of His Passion. Hence, the missionary named the Passion flower. Five blood-colored anthers at the center of the flower suggest the five wounds of Christ. The fringed corona represents the crown of thorns. The stamens form a central column like the cross on which Jesus was scourged, and the stigmas are the nails which impaled Him. Finally, the petals represent the ten apostles present at the Crucifixion (Peter and Judas being absent). Other Spanish settlers were also inspired by the Christic symbolism derived from the plant and named it the Flower of Five Wounds.

The common name May-pop refers to the fruit which forms in late summer. Native Americans used the fruit as a cure for insomnia and some thought it had a calming effect on nervous disorders.

DESCRIPTION

The Passion flower is one of the most beautiful of perennial vines. Grown for its interesting and ornamental flowers, the plant is a vigorous grower and comparatively free of pests. The unusual design of the flower is most interesting, with single or double rows of filaments (the corona) at the base of the flower. Flowers bloom in a mixture of blue, purple, and white, and grow up to 4 inches across on slender stems that grow 20 to 30 feet in length. The stems are covered with small, dark green leaves. The fragrant flowers are followed by fruits the size and shape of a small egg, bright orange in color when ripe. Passion flower blooms from June to September.

CULTIVATION

Plants are moderately easy to grow in warm areas. Hardy through zone 7, the plants perform best in northern areas in pots or tubs. Plants tolerate some frost, to about 30°F. If they die back to the ground, they will often re-emerge if frost has not permeated the roots. Seeds may be sown in spring in average, well-drained soil, but sometimes plants take a couple of years to flower. Fertilize and water regularly. Plants in pots or tubs can be kept growing well for years by top-dressing them each spring with fresh compost. Prune as soon as the plants have finished flowering. Cut them back to about one third of their length, leaving about four buds and thin out weak shoots. The short thin growths should not be pruned; these will bear next year's flowers. Passion flowers climb by means of tendrils; a sturdy support should be provided. They make an excellent winter houseplant.

COMMENTS: May-pop, *Passifloria incarnata*, is native to the United States from Maryland to Florida and west to Texas. Its blooms grow 1½ to 2 inches and the plants bear sweet-tasting, edible fruits. The pods, when stepped upon, pop loudly, hence the common name.

POSITION: Sun or light shade.

PROPAGATION: Seed or cuttings.

Passiflora caerulea (above). *P. incarnata* (opposite).

Trumpet Creeper

Trumpet Vine

Campsis radicans

✺ HISTORY ✺

Trumpet creeper is native to the woodlands of the southern United States, from New Jersey west to Ohio and Iowa, and as far south as Florida and Texas, where it grows in damp woods and along fields. In the 1600s and 1700s, trumpet creeper was originally called jasmine or honeysuckle by the early colonists because it resembled the trumpet-like flowers of those plants. It was imported to Europe around 1640. The name *Campsis* was originally used in 1790 by the Portuguese missionary Juan Loureiro. It is derived from the Greek *kampe*, which means "bending or curved," and refers to the curved stamens as well as the plant's habit of turning towards anything nearby to which it can attach itself. *Radicans* meanas "rooting on or above the ground."

Trumpet creeper was one of the few vines grown by Thomas Jefferson at Monticello. Jefferson recorded it as the Trumpet Flower in his garden notebooks.

DESCRIPTION

These handsome climbing plants are easily recognized by their bright orange or yellow trumpets which bloom from July through September. The showy trumpet flowers are bright orange or orange-scarlet, 2 to 3 inches long and about 2 inches wide. The dark green foliage contrasts well with the abundance of flower clusters. (The yellow form is *C. radicans flava*.) These plants do not have tendrils, but use aerial roots for climbing. Trumpet creeper can grow up to 30 feet or more. Trumpet creeper is a favorite of birds. Hummingbirds will visit regularly for the nectar and northern orioles have been known to feed by pecking a hole through the base of the flower to reach the nectar inside. Trumpet creeper clings to any rough surface. It can be grown in pots and is excellent as a fence climber.

CULTIVATION

The only needs of trumpet creeper are ordinary soil and a sunny spot. It grows easily in a variety of soils, but thrives in open places with fertile soil.

A perennial, trumpet creeper is easiest to purchase as young plants or bare roots from the nursery. If setting it near a building or wall, plant at least 24 inches away, since the roots can penetrate the foundation. Guide the first stems onto a support, then prune back the branches to the trunk in March of each year. The flowers will appear in clusters on the end of the new year's branches.

Fertilize once a year, if at all, and water regularly in hot, dry areas. Give winter protection the first two or three years until the plant is well established. Cuttings taken in spring root easily in sandy soil.

COMMENTS: The Chinese trumpet creeper, *C. grandiflora*, is a very similar plant. It climbs to 20 feet and bears red flowers that bloom in late summer.

POSITION: Sun.

PROPAGATION: Seed or cuttings.

Wisteria

Japanese Wisteria
Wisteria floribunda

Chinese Wisteria
Wisteria sinensis

HISTORY

One of the first Wisterias ever cultivated was from eastern North America, *W. frutescens* was introduced in England in 1724 by Mark Catesby under the unusual name of Carolina Kidney Bean. It was this wisteria that Thomas Jeffererson grew at Monticello. The popularity of this species was soon overtaken by the discovery of the Asiatic species with its magnificent blooms.

In 1816, the Chinese wisteria, *W. sinensis*, was introduced in England. In 1830, Japanese wisteria, *W. floribunda*, was introduced in Europe from Japan.

The first wisteria plant introduce in America was sent to the old Parson's Nursery in Long Island, New York, in 1862.

The American horticulturist Thomas Nuttall named the genus *Wistaria* in 1818 in memory of Caspar Wistar, a German professor of anatomy at the University of Pennsylvania. Because the family spelled their name Wister and Wistar, both names were used for the genus, creating confusion. The more commonly used spelling is *Wisteria*.

DESCRIPTION

Wisteria is one of the most beautiful and easiest to grow of the climbing vines. Chinese wisteria is much faster growing than Japanese wisteria. It climbs to 80 feet or more, and can easily cover walls, arbors, or old trees in a few years. The pea-shaped blooms appear before the leaves, and come in violet-blue, 1-inch long flowers, in dense clusters up to 6 to 12 inches in length. The flowers open all at once and are slightly fragrant. Chinese wisteria blooms earlier, usually mid-May, just after its leaves emerge, and is also available in white and double flowers. Japanese wisteria is a hardier plant than the Chinese. It tolerates lower temperatures, making it the better choice for northern gardens. Its very fra-grant flowers bloom 2 to 3 weeks later than the Chinese, and it has smaller, more widely spaced flowers that open progessively. Flowers are blue or violet-blue, with varieties in white, pink, and double. The ¾-inch flowers bloom in 8- to 24-inch clusters. The pale green leaves can grow up to 15 inches long. Japanese wisteria blooms around late May. It is best for training on a standard. To distinguish Japanese from Chinese wisteria, note the twining habits. Japanese twines in a counterclockwise direction, and Chinese in a clockwise manner around supports. The seeds and pods of both plants are poisonous.

CULTIVATION

Wisteria performs best in a deep, rich soil with lots of organic matter, but will perform in most soils. Plants do not transplant well, so plant wisteria where you want it to grow. Buy new plants in pots from reputable nurseries to ensure blooms, or purchase plants already in bloom, since wisterias can often take several years to flower. Manure heavily the first year to help plants develop more rapidly. Water regularly. For abundant flowering, prune twice a year, first in August and then in late winter or very early spring. In summer, prune new growths to about 12 inches from their branches. In winter, prune back to the second bud, or eye; the new season's flowers will be produced from this point. Be careful to give the plant sufficient climbing space. If restricted to a too-confined space, it can cause considerable structural damage to its support. This can, however, be controlled through systematic pruning. Wisteria is easy to raise from seed, but hybrids will not come true.

POSITION: Sun.

PROPAGATION: Seed, cuttings, layers, or grafting.

Japanese Wisteria (above). Chinese Wisteria (opposite).

INDEX OF BOTANICAL NAMES

INDEX OF ROSES BY CLASSIFICATION

INDEX OF LIGHT- AND PART SHADE-TOLERANT ROSES

'Alfred de Dalmas'
'American Pillar'
'Blanc Double de Coubert'
'Cécile Brunner'
'Dorothy Perkins'
'Félicité Parmentier'
'Gloire de Dijon'

'Harison's Yellow'
'Jacques Cartier'
'Königen von Dänemark'
'Louise Odier'
'Madame Alfred Carriere'
'Madame Hardy'
'Madame Isaac Pereire'

'Old Blush'
'Sombreuil'
Rosa x *centifolia*
'Rosa Mundi'
'Rose du Roi'
'Sir Thomas Lipton'
'Stanwell Perpetual'

INDEX OF ROSES SUITABLE FOR BOTH SHRUBS AND CLIMBING

'Frau Karl Druschki'
'Harison's Yellow'

'Madame Hardy'
'Madame Isaac Periere'

'Old Blush'